Mediation in the Workplace

Mediation in the Workplace

A Guide for Training, Practice, and Administration

Rebecca Jane Weinstein

QUORUM BOOKS
Westport, Connecticut • London

Library of Congress Cataloging-in-Publication Data

Weinstein, Rebecca Jane, 1967–
    Mediation in the workplace : a guide for training, practice, and administration /
Rebecca Jane Weinstein.
        p.   cm.
    Includes bibliographical references and index.
    ISBN 1–56720–336–1 (alk. paper)
    1. Mediation and conciliation, Industrial.   2. Arbitration, Industrial.   I. Title.
HD5481.W43   2001
658.3′154—dc21   00–032820

British Library Cataloguing in Publication Data is available.

Library of Congress Catalog Card Number: 00–032820
ISBN: 1–56720–336–1

First published in 2001

Quorum Books, 88 Post Road West, Westport, CT 06881
An imprint of Greenwood Publishing Group, Inc.
www.quorumbooks.com

Printed in the United States of America

The paper used in this book complies with the
Permanent Paper Standard issued by the National
Information Standards Organization (Z39.48–1984).

10 9 8 7 6 5 4 3 2

This book is dedicated
to my parents.

Contents

Preface

The process of designing and implementing a workplace mediation program requires formulating procedures, training staff mediators, creating oversight committees, educating the workforce, promoting the program, and carrying out mediations. This book is a resource that will assist with all these steps.

Mediation in the Workplace is a guide to mediation theory, with discussions about the most important, as well as some of the most controversial, mediation issues. It reflects on mediation from the standpoint of the workplace and addresses concerns of employers and employees. It is a training guide for the beginning mediator and also a useful reference for the more experienced mediator. This book includes a comprehensive discussion of practice skills as well as individual and interactive training exercises with practice pointers and issues for reflection. This book is also a procedural and administrative guide with a complete set of policies, procedures, and forms, which all can be adopted in entirety or altered to meet the needs of the employer.

Mediation in the Workplace is a valuable tool for both employers and employees; human resource professionals; peer and professional mediation practitioners; mediation instructors and trainers; academics and students in mediation, conflict resolution, business management, public administration, law, social work, counseling, and other related disciplines.

Acknowledgments

A special acknowledgment must be given to my editor and good friend Dr. Jill Ware. Thank you for years of excellent hard work. This book belongs in part to you.

Thank you Ben for your help and friendship and Neal for infiltrating my subconscious.

Also, thank you to my family—my mom Joyce, and my dad Mark, Barbara and Jerry, Nanner and Teddy, Aunt Pearl, Uncle Danny, Lesley, and my brother Jack, for supporting me in many ways. Thank you to my friends Gregory, Laura, Rebecca, and Steve for taking good care of me. Finally, thank you Lisa and Jonathan, I have learned so much from both of you.

I love you all.

Introduction

Mediation is a process in which an impartial third party assists people in conflict to resolve their dispute. Mediation is practical, strategic problem solving that also reflects the emotional and personal needs of the participants. Mediation is both immediately functional and therapeutic. Resolutions designed during mediation aim to produce long-term solutions; they seek to address underlying causes and do not merely address the superficial argument. Mediation also focuses on strengthening relationships and teaching skills that will better equip people to address, or even avoid, conflict in the future.

Mediated resolutions are designed for long-term success without future intervention because complex interpersonal and circumstantial issues are not overlooked in the design. Mediated solutions are not imposed. They are individually formulated to the mutual satisfaction of the parties. And, interestingly, this personalized approach is time-efficient and cost-effective. It is useful in widely diverse settings, less cumbersome than many other conflict resolution processes, and extremely successful. Mediation has been dubbed "miraculous" by some observers, and it is true that to those trapped in a dead-end dispute, mediation may seem like a miracle. It is certainly clear that mediation has proved to be an excellent option for conflict resolution when other traditional approaches have failed.

THE MEDIATOR

Seeking the assistance of an outsider, the mediator, to help resolve a problem or conflict is a common experience to us all. We seek out mediators every day: friends, family, clergy, and personal mentors. These people help us to view complicated and emotional issues with more objectivity and clarity. They help us to gain perspective and see our problems in a new light.

Soliciting the help of people we trust is a natural and normal method of resolving conflict.

One of the reasons we seek out people who know us is that they care about our personal needs: What will happen to the relationship after the conflict is resolved? How will the conflict affect us and the people around us emotionally? Why did the dispute occur in the first place and how can we prevent similar problems from causing us to suffer in the future? When we consult someone with whom we have a personal relationship, we assume they will take into account the issues that are important to us.

These individual and very personal issues are not the top priority of most formalized conflict resolution procedures, such as those within the legal system or the workplace. This is one of the important reasons that we find it unsettling to seek the assistance of lawyers, judges, and work superiors for resolving our conflicts. The solutions they impose are not completely satisfying; they do not reflect our personal concerns.

In contrast, individual and personal issues are a top priority in mediation. Formal mediation is more pragmatic than asking a loved-one for advice, but still requires the mediator to consider and encourage refection on the personal issues. It does not allow a stranger to make decisions for us based on general principles. In mediation, the people involved in the conflict are assisted by an impartial third party who helps to examine and evaluate the issues important to them. Together, the mediator and participants come to a mutually acceptable resolution that solves the problem now and helps to prevent future problems. Informal mediation has been used throughout history because it is effective. Formalized mediation programs are now gaining popularity in numerous arenas, such as within the legal system, communities, schools, and the workplace.

WORKPLACE MEDIATION

Workplace mediation, in particular, can be an effective way to resolve work-related and interpersonal conflicts on the job in a time-efficient and cost-effective manner. Workplace mediation can also help to make the work environment more amicable and less stressful. Empowering workers to reach their own resolutions takes the burden off those who have other priorities; it also strengthens the personal investment that employees have in their jobs.

Workplace mediation is remedial, but it also prevents future disagreement. Conflicts that are resolved amicably and with mutual satisfaction are much less likely to result in more dramatic action—for instance, employing legal or labor union processes. Workplace mediation is a tool for sustaining the growth of the organization and the personal growth of the workers.

In contrast, the traditional method for handling disputes, a grievance procedure, is often punitive in nature. And even when this is not the intent of the employer, employees often perceive the grievance process as a threat. Mediation is based on an entirely different philosophy of problem solving. It is not control-oriented, but rather satisfaction-oriented. At the close of mediation all the people involved have come to a mutual agreement. There are no winners and losers; everyone gains.

Mediation is an appropriate strategy for conflict in most workplace settings. The most important requisite for any mediation program is the employer's interest in adopting mediation. It is not essential that an employer dismantle its traditional grievance procedures. Mediation can be used in conjunction with other programs, as it is in the court and schools systems. Mediation is an alternative, but does not have to be a wholesale substitute. A workplace mediation program should be independent from other grievance processes, with a clear structure and comprehensive policies and procedures. And a mediation program should be implemented for the mutual benefit of the workers and the employer.

ORGANIZATION SIZE

Virtually any workplace can institute a mediation program in which peer or coworker mediators volunteer their services to help resolve disputes. A typical institution that would adopt mediation is a moderate-to-large size organization with a workforce of 100 or more employees. Both for-profit and nonprofit organizations are similarly good candidates.

Larger organizations will house enough staff to create a pool of mediators and an oversight board that are not closely linked to all the other employees. This permits mediation participants to be able to select a mediator with whom they do not work closely.

Smaller organizations can also implement peer mediation programs by networking with other small organizations. A pool of mediators can be created from a number of local groups that are all interested in this form of dispute resolution. When people from one business are involved in a conflict, they simply call on a mediator from outside their own workplace. This works extremely well for training, administration, and practice. Several small firms can organize their mediation program in conjunction with each other; pooling energy saves the time and cost required to design each program independently.

Of course, an organization of any size can implement a mediation program and hire external professional mediators rather than using peer mediators. All organizations, regardless of size, might also consider peer mediation for most day-to-day issues, but reserve outside professional mediators for those concerns that are beyond the capabilities of nonprofessionals. The cost, both financial and not directly monetary, of hiring a professional mediator who successfully resolves a case in several hours is dramatically lower than that of a case escalated to legal action.

UNIONIZED ORGANIZATIONS

Mediation is an excellent tool for both nonunion and union represented organizations. The union shop might initially hesitate to incorporate mediation into its grievance process, but this is a shortsighted view. No union has an unlimited amount of time and funds to address every issue that troubles their members on a day-to-day basis. Unions generally become involved in a conflict when there is the perception of a severe injustice, an important principle is involved, or if there may be a great impact on a large number of members. Unions do not typically intervene in everyday interpersonal squabbles. Issues that involve poor communication or other concerns, while important to the workers, do not rise to the level of union involvement.

Mediation is an opportunity for unions to remove themselves from dilemmas that they perceive as trivial, but cause distress to workers. Union shops who embrace mediation have more time and money to focus on their primary concerns, the fundamental issues for which their membership pay dues. Mediation does not have to be a substitute for any other grievance process, and no resolution should ever be forced during mediation.

At present, there are a number of private and governmental unionized organizations that have adopted mediation. These programs often permit a union representative to be present during the mediation session if the parties so choose. Of course, it is also appropriate to postpone finalization of mediation agreement until after it is reviewed by a union representative. It is important to remember that all conversations that occur during mediation are confidential. For the union, mediation offers the best of both worlds, freedom from the burden of becoming entrenched in day-to-day conflict, and the right to approve or rescind agreements if need be.

MEDIATION AND CONTROL

Mediation is a viable option for virtually every workplace. It is an opportunity for the employer to demonstrate a commitment to its workers, their satisfaction and peace of mind, while benefiting from the resulting increased productivity of a nonconflictual environment. In implementing a mediation process the employer may fear some loss of control, since the workers will be settling their problems autonomously. But anytime there is chaos as a result of conflict in the workplace, there is a loss of control. True control comes with an organized and efficient work environment. The dissatisfaction that often follows traditional grievance procedures results in an underlying chaos that cannot be managed through paternalistic control. When there is discontent that leads to low productivity, high turnover, and a general disquiet, the employer is not in control. Nonetheless, every workplace mediation program should recognize those types of cases that, according to policy, will be addressed through more traditional methods. For instance, violence on the job resulting in injury may be automatically excluded from mediation.

Additionally, when creating agreements, employees should still be required to adhere to the specific policies of the workplace. Although mediation should not overrule fundamental workplace policies and procedures, mediation will be more effective if the employer is willing to be flexible in permitting workers to design resolutions that work for them. However, similar to mediation within the courts, there are mediated agreements that a court will simply not accept. For instance, a court is unlikely to accept mediated agreements related to violent crime.

Mediation is a creative process that aims to design individual and mutually satisfying agreements, but it is not a license for anarchy. Employers should not fear this new mediation philosophy; while certainly different from a traditional patriarchal system, mediation is designed to improve the workplace for employees and employers alike.

Section I

THEORY AND PRACTICE

Part One

Mediation Discussion

Conflict

Conflict is the interpersonal response to a threatening event: when feelings of frustration or anger rise beyond control, a conflict ensues. Conflict is an ultimate act: it marks the end of a path. Conflict is an opening: it presents an opportunity to move beyond a problem. Conflict is the sign that resolution is needed: to resolve conflict, history must be addressed and perceptions must be changed. The resolution of conflict is a release and a closure.

CONFLICT IN THE WORK SETTING

All conflict, whether in a personal or professional setting, involves emotional response. Viewing conflict from an emotional perspective is a logical and common interpretation in private matters. But, in the workplace, it may contradict fundamental beliefs about propriety and professional behavior.

There are a number of reasons why people do not express themselves in emotional terms on the job. Expressing emotion in a professional setting is perceived as inappropriate. The job site is not a place for free expression of feelings. Responding with emotion comes across as childish and self-centered. It may demonstrate that one's focus is on personal satisfaction rather than accomplishing group goals. Emotion is often associated with irrational behavior and a loss of control. For men, emotion may be perceived as weak and feminine. Women may avoid emotional responses so as not to project negative stereotypes.

Despite the fact that people avoid emotionally expressive language in the workplace, people still respond emotionally. In reporting responses to situations some people use words that clearly describe feelings, such as "I am angry" or "I was humiliated." There is no question that these descriptions indicate an emotional response. However, open expressions such as these are often reserved for friends or escape only during heated moments, with ensuing regret.

It is important not to confuse lack of expression with lack of feeling. Some people are more ready to express feelings than others, and herein lies the problem. Since all people are personally and emotionally affected by the world around them, these feelings, when not openly expressed, may vent in nonproductive ways. Typical outlets for emotions unexpressed on the job are gossip, backstabbing, wasting time, misusing sick leave, expressing negativity, and abusing authority. All of these forms of passive-aggressive behavior have real repercussions for employees and employers. Because people are not accustomed to expressing their emotions at work, they may not even be aware of their underlying feelings and the ways in which these feelings can affect their behavior.

Take, for example, this scenario: Two colleagues are writing a joint report. A conflict arises over a morning deadline. One person has a family and must get home for dinner; he is willing to suffer the consequences of submitting a late report. The other person is single and would rather work all night; for her, losing face by handing in a late report is unacceptable. Assume that they resolve the conflict amicably: The single person stays late alone, and the married person agrees to take responsibility for the next project.

It is true that the conflict was resolved in a rational manner, and ideally there will be no further repercussions. Consider, though, what feelings might be occurring. The married man wants to be with his family; he loves to eat dinner with his children, and his wife is not pleased when he comes home late. He feels pressures from all sides; he resents the self-centered attitude of his colleague but also feels a sense of shame from not fulfilling his work duties. He knows his work suffers because of his private life and is embarrassed that, as a result of his personal choices, colleagues look down on his performance.

The single person is frustrated and resentful that someone else has the power to dictate what might happen to her on the job. Her priorities are with her work. She is angered that the extra burden must fall on her shoulders, and, if the work is not completed, she will be punished. She feels she is in a bind: either complete the work that belongs to someone else or put her own career in jeopardy.

Even though an agreement has been made, there is a good chance that resentment and lack of trust will follow this relationship to the next assignment because none of the underlying feelings have been expressed. Overlooking the real emotions that arise as a function conflict is shortsighted. However, simply recognizing that emotion underlies all conflict does not reduce the cultural taboo against expressing emotion in the workplace. Since emotion is so hidden on the job, its expression often takes inappropriate forms, such as angry explosions, backstabbing, or hurtful gossip. People are simply not socialized or properly educated in how to express honest emotion in appropriate ways on the job.

It is important to note that recognizing and addressing emotion is not a license to disregard tact. It is also not an invitation for the workplace to become an open forum for dramatic emotional outbursts. Accepting the reality that emotions influence behavior in significant ways, and feed conflict, is a strategy for initiating real change, not a suggestion to forgo professionalism for theatrics. The concept, to encourage overt or underlying emotions to be expressed, but in a manner that allows rational response to these expressions, is an attempt to more fully address the emotional repercussions of conflict.

DYSFUNCTIONAL CONFLICT MANAGEMENT

Instead of developing safe and effective avenues to express emotion at work, complicated power games are created that afford an outlet for emotional energy. Rather than acknowledging that emotional responses are healthy and necessary, and affirming that conflict is an opportunity for communication, convoluted power struggles emerge.

Conflict is undeniably threatening and often very difficult to face directly. Suggesting that conflict should be used as an outlet for growth presupposes that people have the skills and desire to explore that route. Before being able to generate conflict management strategies that address emotion in functional ways, preconceptions about conflict must be examined to determine in which ways they are dysfunctional.

Power and the Win/Lose Perspective

Very often, conflict is conceptualized from a power perspective. Power is equated with aggression, force, and ultimately winning. Although this is an emotional perspective as well, involving intimidation and fear, here power is seen as a weapon. When conflict is handled using power as a weapon, it accepts the notion that there will be a winner and a loser. The power perspective leaves little room to maneuver, except by force.

Since it is difficult for two opponents to both maintain power, there is always risk. Although it is possible to win a power battle, it is also possible to lose. When the battle is lost, the power is lost, resulting in weakness. In this play, one side is inevitably sacrificed. Additionally, a single power struggle usually leads to another; either the loser or another opponent will vie for control. Regardless who wins or loses in a battle for power, both sides expend tremendous energy and are forced to sacrifice.

Does the winner have more to gain if the opponent loses? This may be true in all-or-nothing situations, but in the average workplace, winning is a group effort. In some situations there will be winners and losers on the job—in promotion, for example. But typical work conflicts involve interpersonal frustrations, issues of respect, fairness, acknowledgment, and having a voice. The concept of survival of the fittest just isn't relevant.

This combative representation of power suggests two warriors, and many people do enjoy a high-stakes game. For most people though, the risk of losing is far too serious to turn conflict into a power game. In the average workplace relationship, conflict is less about wielding power in order to destroy others, and more about getting through the day with a job, dignity, and sanity intact. Power is about having a voice, gaining respect, and achieving success that does not come at the expense of others. For those people who are not willing to kill or be killed, it makes more sense to reinterpret conflict, separate it from aggressive power, and plan a strategy that includes responding to underlying emotion and finding emotionally satisfying solutions to problems.

Taking emotion into consideration when responding to conflict does not require denying that a power play exists. It is inherent in conflict that strengths and weaknesses will be explored. But there is a great difference between usurping power from others and being personally empowered oneself. One person does not have to be weak for another to be strong. In most situations, each person involved in a dispute will possess some power. Power comes in many forms.

Passive and Aggressive Bargaining

Power relationships are affected by the style in which people respond to conflict. A passive approach to conflict resolution can have an equally strong impact as an aggressive approach. Both styles can be effective, and both can also be abused. Either style can be employed to intimidate or manipulate.

Passivity lends itself to accommodation. A passive stance may be an attempt to discourage aggression from an opponent; in a battle, an aggressive person may win by sheer force. In an aggressive stance, adamant positions are taken regardless of the potential costs. This approach may bring success if an opponent concedes, but if an impasse occurs, both sides lose.

Passive and aggressive bargaining both involve risk. When unequivocal positions are taken, there is less control over the outcome. When steadfast about a position, compromise is unlikely. Preoccupation with a viewpoint forfeits the opportunity to examine more subtle desires and intentions. Also, a stubborn attitude may provoke more resistance in an opponent. This type of posturing always results in a loser.

Passivity can have similar results. Refusing to take a position can also be interpreted as an absolute stance. Although it may be easy to take advantage of a passive person, it may also be very difficult to negotiate with a person who refuses to actively participate. An impasse due to passive bargaining is equally destructive to the relationship.

What is most detrimental, however, is when passive and aggressive bargaining is dishonest. It exaggerates positions and obscures true intentions.

Deceptive posturing hinders honest negotiations and leads to dissatisfaction. When taking an exaggerated position, the most that can be expected is reaching the midpoint between the two positions. The act of overstating for the purpose of haggling presupposes that the middle ground will be accepted. True needs or desires are obscured. In the end, each party walks away having less than demanded; the result is always a loser.

The Impact of Context on Strategy

Circumstances greatly affect bargaining strategies. Behavior and conflict style will be impacted by the context of the relationship. For instance, a forty-year-old man will bargain differently with his eight-year-old son than with his supervisor at work, although these two relationships influence each other.

Imagine that the man has an authoritarian supervisor; there is little room for compromise or error at work. At work the man is powerless. When he returns home, he is tired and demoralized. But now, between himself and his eight year old, he has power. He behaves toward his son as his boss did with him; he tolerates little compromise or error. Perhaps this response is a direct result of feeling powerless at work, or possibly he recognizes that aggressive authority is a very effective form of control. Now consider the man's wife. She is neither a superior nor a subordinate. The man's bargaining style with his wife is a reflection of additional variables. He is neither powerful nor powerless and must adapt his manner again.

Whatever the specific variables, a person cannot be separated from his or her circumstances. Conflict always has a context. Reactions to conflict always occur within a context and reflect an individual's circumstances. This context can be identified and a response can be designed accordingly.

The strategy chosen for dealing with conflict should be conscious and deliberate. The method should reflect the most appropriate style for any given set of variables in a particular context.

FUNCTIONAL CONFLICT MANAGEMENT

Conflict resolution should be conceived to resolve conflict, not merely change its form. Strategy, unlike a win/lose power struggle, does not demand capitalizing on secrecy, deception, or manipulation. Rather than to deceive and conquer, the strategic goal can be to redirect, reconceptualize, or redefine.

Instead of equating conflict with battle and aggressive power, it is possible to view conflict as a dance. Dance is a series of intertwined steps, passionate and reflective or heated and reactive. Dance can be both choreographed and improvised. To choreograph indicates planned control; to improvise manifests flexibility and freedom. Productive conflict resolution does not deny control, it permits planning and strategy. It also embraces emotion, is tolerant of change, accepts mistakes but attempts to correct them, and is a collaborative effort.

During a dispute, choices are made about how time and energy will be expended. A power battle is all consuming and assumes loss. Since the goal is to win, the focus is on defeating the opponent. There is little room for objective evaluation of the problem and mutual organization of a solution. In contrast, joining together to address a problem as a collaborative effort unveils the possibility of mutual satisfaction. Accepting the emotional nature of conflict permits thorough exploration and helps to heal wounds that may infect a relationship. Personal empowerment does not rob others of their rightful position and breeds respect rather then contempt. Conflict can lead to strength, personally and interpersonally. Opening that possibility is a choice.

Styles of Conflict Management

The way in which individuals behave during conflict depends on personality, experience, training, and the particular circumstances of the situation. Although predicting behavior is difficult, past patterns inform future conduct. All people demonstrate responses that for them are familiar and comfortable. Some of these habitual responses will prove successful over time and others will generate repeated disruption. Recognizing commonly successful strategies, and those that cause frustration, is a useful step in learning to modify behavior and improve satisfaction. Developing the ability to resolve conflict in a strategic fashion helps to increase contentment and decrease stress.

Conflict resolution styles can be labeled and distinguished. Differentiating these styles aids in recognizing and predicting behavior. Recognizing styles helps to identify the tendencies people display. These clearly delineated styles are not a precise reflection of the strategies people adopt, however; most actual behavior reveals a combination of conflict resolution styles.

While it is impossible to control the behavior of other people, personal behavior can be adapted to help direct communication. If an opponent is behaving in an adversarial manner, responding with a collaborative or accommodating approach may bring to light an alternative perspective. Strategic thinkers aim to meld styles that work together rather than repel.

A mediator who is aware of his or her own tendencies and motivations may have clearer insight into the perspectives of others. People do not always respond in predictable ways. For instance, people who are generally passive may become quite assertive during a conflict. The motivation for particular behavior is not always apparent. A collaborative approach may be used as a means to deceive. No one conflict resolution style is ideal in every situation.

In designing strategies for resolving conflict, it is useful to identify motivation. Identifying the reason for a particular response can be instructive. Preparing a strategy offers some direction. It is important for mediators to model productive techniques in order to educate parties as to how adjustments to their behavior might produce desirable outcomes.

The following presents general categories of conflict resolution styles. Many more subcategories or combined categories exist. This is merely a guide for recognizing common strategies familiar to many people.

COMPETITIVE

This is an aggressive stance in which winning tends to be linked to self-worth. A competitive person enjoys argument and the feeling of power associated with defeating an opponent. Those who enjoy competition in work may also enjoy the thrill of battle in interpersonal relationships.

A competitive person is not necessarily aggressive or adversarial, although a competitive attitude may be perceived this way. Competitiveness evokes ambivalent responses. Although competitive behavior is often promoted and revered, such as in sports and business, it is also disdained in interpersonal relationships. People who are competitive are perceived either as strong, competent, and independent or as insecure, hostile, and self-involved.

Many people do have a competitive nature but attempt to disguise it in order to appear more team-oriented. In the workplace a contradiction emerges where there is pressure to be both a team player and highly competitive. Additional confusion results when it is not clear which circumstances call for which approach. Given this paradox, some people act as a team player for the purpose of self-promotion. This behavior supports the group, but the underlying motivation is competitive.

Competition also carries an element of thrill and adventure. Many people view competition as sport. They have no intention of harming others. They simply enjoy the thrill of the game. For those who do not share this perception, competitive people can be quite threatening. A noncompetitive person may shrink in the company of the highly competitive. The motivation of a competitive person may also be misinterpreted, eliciting an aggressive response out of self-defense.

ADVERSARIAL

This tendency involves taking strong and adamant positions regardless of the value of other perspectives. Adversarial relationships are often perceived as less personal or emotional and more rational. Deliberate strategy is employed to advance an interpretation or a plan of action. "Justice" is often the rationale for engaging in adversarial tactics.

The most common reference for adversarial action is the legal system, which is described as an "adversarial system." An adversarial approach is different from a competitive approach in that adversaries take absolute positions based on an interpretation of the problem. Although competition may be perceived as a battle of might, adversaries battle using wit. Adversaries may take positions that they do not fully believe, but that serve to strengthen their point. Those who adopt the adversarial approach are often advocates for a cause.

There are few arenas where the adversarial approach is productive. To fully engage an adversarial philosophy, the opponents must be willing to either sacrifice all other aspects of the relationship or remove themselves emotionally from the battle. A curious phenomenon occurs, for instance, when lawyers can engage in a heated argument that appears to stem from deeply held beliefs and moments later they are friendly and harbor no ill will. This is possible because lawyers take positions that are based on ideas, not emotions.

While lawyers certainly feel, professionally they remove themselves from this sentiment and argue the case as necessary. This is a difficult strategy for people who are personally connected to a problem. For this reason, even lawyers will not handle their own legal matters. From an adversarial perspective, emotion clouds judgment.

COLLABORATIVE

This style employs teamwork and cooperation to meet some mutually acceptable goal. Various perspectives are examined and the sides come together with a patchwork solution. Collaboration may be difficult to sustain in highly emotional situations.

Collaboration tends to be the approach perceived as the most honorable and productive, and when true collaboration is possible it is a satisfying way to work. However, idealizing this technique disregards the fact that a dispute makes collaborating inherently difficult. Collaboration requires interaction that is basically free from conflict. In collaboration people are able to put their own needs aside for the common good—or at least prioritize the common good over their own needs. Collaboration requires teamwork and an ability to view issues objectively.

Perhaps it is possible for some people to work jointly from a shared perspective to resolve conflict, but it requires great maturity and self-control. When collaboration is attempted for resolving disputes, controversies may remain under the surface.

Often, collaboration is an admirable objective and an excellent way to prevent conflict from occurring at the outset. Shared perspectives, teamwork, and mutual concern and respect are goals to strive for in all interpersonal relationships, business or private. But when people are bogged down with frustration, anger, resentment, confusion, fear, or any other emotions typically associated with conflict, the amicable relationship necessary for collaboration may be difficult to attain.

Many discussions on mediation identify collaboration as the ideal strategy for dispute resolution. Some practitioners suggest that the mediator aim to initiate collaborative efforts and that collaboration is the heart of mediation. In part this is true. Collaboration involves coming together to work toward a mutually defined end. All interaction during mediation can be viewed as collaboration. This interpretation can be very uplifting to the parties. People come to mediation in turmoil. Offering collaboration as an alternative response may bring a sense of relief and can lead to productive work, even if the parties are unable to collaborate consistently throughout the process.

ACCOMMODATING

Although cooperation is necessary in accommodation, sometimes accommodation occurs despite a desire to act differently. Accommodating consists of capitulating in order to gain or maintain something else of value. Accommodating can be productive in smoothing the way to a solution. However, accommodating can become acquiescing, which can be used to appease or manipulate, leaving the problem yet unsolved.

In many instances accommodation is a positive step and necessary for compromise. Conflicts often arise from the perception that there is a lack of simple accommodation. Resolving conflict often hinges on small accommodations. From this perspective, accommodation is a necessary part of most resolution.

However, when accommodating is perceived as succumbing, resentments can build. The accommodating person may feel used or disregard feeling they are weak, nonassertive, and perhaps manipulated. The person being accommodated may feel that the gesture was insincere, that a hidden agenda will be revealed in the future. Trust in the agreement is put at risk if questionable accommodations are made.

Although accommodation is a necessary part of compromise and problem solving, caution should be taken so that the agreement is not precarious. Accommodation may also be used to avoid dealing with a painful, stressful, or an otherwise difficult situation. Conflict resolution should aim to resolve the entirety of the problem, not mask the issues with a short-lived feel-good agreement.

PROBLEM SOLVING

Similar to collaborating, problem solving involves focusing on a question and its answer. It is a more formal process than other types of collaboration, often employing organized protocol for examining a problem, investigating options, and initiating a planned solution.

Problem solving is often associated with a more scientific or systematic approach. It is related to an adversarial strategy in that positions are taken and arguments are made, but they are examined cooperatively, not competitively. Problem solving is a composite of several approaches. It is both rational and collaborative.

However, problem solving may be too clinical for issues that are subjective or emotionally charged. The scientific examination of a problem will usually lead to a practical resolution, one that is just and effective, but may not satisfy passions. Successful problem solving must reflect personal perceptions. People who consider themselves strongly rational are often at odds with the highly emotional, since each is sensitive to the flaws in the others' approach.

Imposing strict problem-solving techniques is a common mistake of inexperienced mediators. The mediator inquires as to what each side wants, and then attempts to reach a compromised middle ground. This is an effective way to reach a settlement, but it will not usually be honored. Conflict is more complex than this approach acknowledges.

Problem solving, while clinical and emotionally removed, is an excellent tool for examining issues and gaining perspective. For those who are entangled in emotions or unable to view perspectives other than their own, assessing issues in a clinical manner can be very informative and help to dispel biases that make agreement difficult.

COMPROMISE

Like cooperation, compromise can be used as a way to avoid conflict and satisfy others' needs at one's own cost. A compromise strategy assumes that no one will get everything they desire. If both sides compromise, an acceptable middle ground can often be reached. If only one side will compromise, unfair advantage may be taken.

Compromise is very much like accommodation, but suggests that both sides have made accommodations after mutual agreement. Compromise is an integral part of most agreements. Whether the negotiations were held in a competitive, collaborative, or problem-solving manner, ultimately both sides make compromises. Even when receiving everything requested, the act of negotiating often feels like a compromise, particularly if negotiations have been difficult or stressful.

Compromise is subjective. There are clear compromises, such as dividing money in half, but compromise often reflects personal perceptions. Inexperienced mediators sometimes attempt to initiate a compromise that appears equal from an objective standpoint, when fair agreements from the perspective of the parties are often based on subjective assessments of fairness. It is often the willingness to compromise that is most important to the process, not the specifics of the agreement. Movement away from rigid positions opens the door for resolution. The act of compromise can be cathartic for those who have felt constrained by disagreement.

Since compromise is such an important part of the resolution process, it is tempting to prematurely pressure the parties into compromise. However, there is little point in instigating compromise when the parties have not independently reached that step in the process. A compromised agreement that is created with uncertainty will doubtfully withstand time.

AVOIDING

This style can be either passive or aggressive. Avoiding, as a rule, halts a process. This can stifle an opponent. Avoiding can occur as a response to intimidation or aggressive manipulation or it may indicate a simple desire to postpone conflict until a more appropriate time.

Avoiding is a common tactic people use to deal with conflict. The prospect of dealing directly with conflict is overwhelming, so the natural response is to do nothing. This is not a bad strategy in many cases. Waiting for anger or pain to subside, for the prominence of the issue to wane, is often a sufficient catalyst for resolution. In some instances time simply erases the problem, but in other cases time offers only the illusion of resolve. A problem ignored may appear to be forgotten, but underlying concerns still remain. Dredging up these buried issues may be a useful exercise, but it depends on the nature of the problem, the relationship of the people, and their goals. It may, or may not, be worth the effort it takes to work through repressed feelings.

In other situations, avoiding can be a wholly inadequate and unproductive way of handling conflict. Sometimes avoidance is used to intimidate, manipulate, or harass. If one person actively avoids a problem, it requires significant assertion and bravery for another person to press the issue. Avoidance can also increase the magnitude of the dilemma in people's minds. It may exaggerate the intensity of positions and feelings. Problems often get worse when ignored.

Avoiding a confrontation also may increase rumination on a problem. When one person insists on avoiding confrontation, the other person remains trapped in their own thoughts. This is a very effective way to manipulate. It can be cruel to disregard a person when it is clear they are upset. The motivation for this disregard may be fear, intimidation, pain, anger, or an otherwise legitimate feeling, but the person left to wallow in a problem can feel quite trapped.

Mediation is a method of conflict resolution that is very sensitive to the consequences of avoidance. People often come to mediation after a long period of avoiding a problem. Mediation is specifically designed to be a safe and comfortable arena for addressing issues that have been avoided. Relevant issues rarely remain untouched in the course of mediation.

Mediated Disputes

Mediation is a unique and exceptional way of handling disputes. It combines the practical features of problem solving and negotiation with a focus on personal concerns. While mediation serves to solve problems by developing coherent strategies through agreements or contracts, it also aids in building better communication and addresses how people feel about their circumstances. Mediation adds a human element to conflict resolution that is missing from other formal conflict resolution. This humanistic perspective is particularly important because most other resolution processes neglect to recognize the personal or emotional element in all conflicts.

Disruptions in our lives in the form of conflict affect us as people. Whether the conflict surrounds business negotiations, contract disputes, team projects at work, an argument between coworkers, or simple day-to-day frustrations, we cannot separate our personal selves from our experiences, even when those experiences involve issues entirely business-related. Mediation has proven to be overwhelmingly successful because it embraces two equally important aspects of problem solving: the need to formally resolve issues with a mutually satisfying concrete plan, and the need to address the emotional aspects of conflict.

Mediation promotes agreements that address the underlying concerns that caused the conflict to occur in the first place. In addition, mediation addresses the future of the relationship. No agreement can withstand the strain of people who cannot, or will not, adhere to the agreement. If there is little professional, personal, or emotional comfort with the agreement, the agreement is not worth the paper it is printed on and certainly more conflict will follow. Mediation seeks to do more than resolve the apparent conflict; it seeks to prevent further conflict. Its aim is to strengthen relationships, build communication skills, quell feelings of fear, and teach more productive techniques for interaction in both the business and personal realms.

Mediation is a highly practical tool. It is less cumbersome and costly than other formal conflict resolution processes, and it does not require an inordinate amount of time or emotional commitment. Mediation is ideal for those business, workplace, or interpersonal disputes that should not be relegated to the enormously complex legal system. In fact, a great many disputes that have plodded through the legal system for years are settled by mediation in a matter of hours, saving countless dollars and enormous amounts of time and stress.

Mediation is also excellent for those business, workplace, or interpersonal disputes that affect people in emotional or personal ways, disputes that the legal system is ill equipped to handle. Work-related disputes affected by personal feelings and perceptions, not appropriate for the legal system, are also not properly addressed through counseling or therapy. Mediation is an opportunity to handle conflict in a strategic manner while respecting emotional undercurrents.

GRIEVANCE PROCEDURES

Mediation differs from the traditional grievance process in the workplace. Most grievance procedures are loosely based on the legal or adversarial system. They are highly structured and rule based. There is a finder of fact and a person, or series of people, who have the authority to make determinations based on facts and procedure. While the typical grievance procedure may serve the important function in the workplace of maintaining control, it is rarely tailored to the particular needs and circumstances of any given problem. As a result, grievance procedures are widely disliked by employees and management alike.

There is frequently a sense, whether justified or unjustified, that workplace grievance procedures are unfair and burdensome. Employees feel threatened by what is perceived as a no-win situation, and management is hindered with an obligation to use punitive measures to maintain order. In a workplace, where settling disputes is essential for productive ongoing relationships, a flawed grievance process can do far more harm than good. As in the legal system, mediation is an excellent alternative in the workplace for problem solving that lends itself to workable agreements that are mutually satisfying.

BENEFITS OF MEDIATION

Mediation is a simple process. In mediation an impartial third party assists the disputing people to reach a mutually acceptable resolution. The mediator does not act as a judge or advocate. The rules of the legal system do not apply. Mediation is a creative process. The parties are free to design a solution that is effective and satisfying from their perspective, rather than being judged by the perceptions of outsiders. The parties are not limited by rules of law or precedents designed for general problems, but not for this specific problem.

Mediation is a thorough process. The parties are invited to examine the issues that instigated the dispute. They are encouraged to consider what effect the conflict has on their professional and personal lives. The parties also explore the potential outcome, designing a resolution that will resolve the negative effects experienced from the conflict and thwart future negative effects. Mediation is preventive. Time is spent formulating an agreement that can realistically be fulfilled without further intervention. Mediation promotes long-term solutions

Mediation allows the people involved in a conflict to address each other directly rather then through an advocate. By speaking openly, miscommunication and misunderstandings are more likely to be revealed and dispelled. Attention may be focused on any nuance of the dispute they wish. They are not confined by bureaucratic rules. The parties may explore emotions and personal perceptions. Mediation promotes emotional healing and personal satisfaction.

Finally, mediation is accessible and cost-effective. It is less expensive and time-consuming than employing many other conflict resolution processes. Mediation is completed within hours rather then months or years. Mediation offers the average person a much needed opportunity for the timely and efficient resolution of disputes.

Cost Benefits of Mediation

Compared to litigation, mediation can save time and money. To the trepidation of many, conflicts often take a dramatic route and enter the morass of the legal system. Regardless of where the conflict begins, in the workplace, in the community, or in the home, conflicts that are not resolved by the people involved often become a legal action. The typical cost of a lawsuit will vary, but within the legal system an apparently minor complaint often becomes enormously expensive and time-consuming, a common fear for every employer. Mediation can counter these costs. It is estimated that an average of 50 percent of advanced legal cases transferred to mediation are resolved in less than one day.

Workplace disputes have additional costs beyond the monetary threat of a lawsuit. Disputes on the job hamper productivity and morale. Dissatisfied workers have a higher turnover rate, thus requiring retraining and burdening experienced workers. Workplace conflict promotes destructive gossip, breeding fear and distrust. Without adequate ways to address the daily concerns of the workers and management, frustrations build, leading to added conflict. While mediation may not replace other formal grievance procedures, mediation can benefit the workplace as it benefits the legal system. It offers a desperately needed alternative that is cost-effective and time-efficient.

ROLES OF THE MEDIATOR

Although mediation is informed by the legal and counseling disciplines, it is neither a highly structured legalistic process nor is it emotionally draining and intrusive therapy. Mediation does incorporate the appropriate and most useful tools from each field. Mediation employs organized and deliberate problem solving while allowing a needed therapeutic outlet. Mediation extends to the parties a nonthreatening and private arena to discuss issues openly without the threat of retribution. A mediator assists as a nonjudgmental objective outsider. The mediator maintains the control and provides the structure needed to protect the parties from any chaos resulting from confrontation. Mediation can be facilitated by a professional mediator or a peer mediator. Both types of mediators can be very successful.

The mediator has two primary roles: facilitator and coordinator. As a facilitator, the mediator assists in drawing out information from one person and fostering the understanding of that information by another person. Much of the focus of mediation is placed on the issues that caused the conflict. Through group discussion and private meetings with the mediator, the parties are encouraged to examine the elements that compose the conflict. This may require reflection on the work environment, interpersonal communication, and work and personal stressors.

By asking questions, the mediator assists the parties to understand the nuances of the conflict, design a strategy for resolving this particular conflict, and prevent future conflicts. As a facilitator who has the benefit of unencumbered insight, the mediator can offer a perspective that is new to the parties. The mediator assists the parties to move beyond the view they have of the problem and their preconceived resolutions. Creative solutions that are generated by the parties, with the facilitation of the mediator, are often novel and address underlying concerns that the parties did not realize were affecting the relationship and hindering resolution.

The mediator is also a coordinator. The mediator helps to direct the flow of the session and assists the parties to set boundaries. Mediation is relatively unstructured, tolerant of open discourse and a certain degree of emotional expression. However, mediation still maintains a professional and organized framework. Mediation is not a chaotic free-for-all. In fact, one of the benefits of mediation is that it reins in much of the chaos that plagues ordinary efforts to communicate. Mediation escapes the rigidity of many other formal resolution processes, but maintains a rational and productive working environment.

MEDIATION VERSUS THE ADVERSARIAL MODEL

Adversarial Position Taking

People involved in disputes benefit from the assistance of a mediator, as conflict commonly leads to a myopic view. During conflict, people often see only their own perspective. Frequently, a single-minded view of the issue is the problem itself, the impetus for the dispute. There are various reasons for this limited thinking. Single-mindedness may result from a lack of empathy or it may stem from a lack of opportunity to learn another perspective. Either due to anger or defensiveness, exploring all sides of the issue with an opponent is difficult.

Once entrenched in a dispute, a linear approach strengthens arguments as each side attempts to persuade the other. This is the heart of the adversarial model, to first form a position and then support that position with evidence. This method tends to muddle the initial conflict. It is easy to sacrifice the original objectives or the true interests of the people involved while building an argument. The desire to win can override many of the other moral, political, and personal beliefs held dear.

Position taking and the need to prevail is a great motivator. It inspires the mental and emotional energy necessary to fight for justice. There are times when belief in a position or a cause is extremely important for building the momentum needed to fight a battle. Disputing in an adversarial manner is hard work and to justify it one must hold tightly to one's position. There are appropriate times and places for this type of linear thinking. In most workplace disputes, and even in the average legal dispute, it is questionable whether the people involved will personally benefit from this type of battle mentality.

The battle stances that people take when they are disputing make any real communication difficult, if not impossible. Often, the most gained from hearing an opponent's position is a clearer view of what must be disproved. Gaining a sense of empathy or discovering where the positions converge is difficult. When locked in battle, people are blocked from hearing what they do not wish to hear. This makes reflecting on or internalizing another point of view impossible. An alternative view is no more than a tool that can be used to strengthen a defense. These are not circumstances likely to produce satisfactory resolutions or the enhancement of relationships.

The Effect of Mediation

In mediation the adversarial or position-taking model of dispute is restrained. The parties agree to come to mediation in good faith. They are required to acknowledge the concerns of others; differing perspectives are genuinely considered. The mediator need not employ controlling tactics to promote this type of interaction because the parties agree to a nonadversarial approach. Through reframing, asking questions, and presenting alternatives, the mediator is able to redirect adversarial patterns and sway the parties toward a more cooperative approach to problem solving. If the parties are unwilling or unable to proceed with mediation on these terms, the session ceases. However, mediation is rarely thwarted because people are unwilling to participate honorably in an exploration of the issues.

In working toward a more holistic view of the conflict, perceptions frequently change. When confronted with new information and new perspectives, the parties often support notions that they once strongly opposed. In part, this stems from the fact that humans are inherently contradictory and inconsistent. People are quite adept at switching sides, and often do so with little awareness. This does not imply that people are confused or dishonest, but rather that each person plays many roles in life. This shifting of roles is the key to success.

In most disputes, if the circumstances were slightly altered, each person could easily switch places and argue the other side. This leads to the notion that history, and the way people perceive truth, reflects the stories people tell themselves. When stories change, the perception of reality changes. Understanding life, relationships, and the human experience is a process, a continuum. In mediation, the parties redefine their stories about the conflict and create a new story that is mutually satisfying.

This does not suggest that people must sacrifice their beliefs in order to compromise and reach mutual resolutions. Instead, they merely have to be willing to accept that another point of view exists. Once another point of view is acknowledged, position taking, being absolutely right, is no longer the goal. Absolute rightness and wrongness are much more difficult beliefs to maintain than notions that accept a grey area. When people are freed from the battle, they genuinely desire a meeting of the minds. They understand and embrace the notion that to settle a dispute, there must be some compromise. Even when a sense of rightness remains, the desire to resolve conflict overpowers the need to be vindicated. And in many cases, when other perspectives come to light, each opponent realizes that neither side is completely in the right.

Working toward understanding alternative perspectives, cooperation, and compromise is particularly valuable when the parties in dispute have an on-going relationship. When there is no risk of future confrontation, position taking is easier to maintain. But when further communication is required, the parties often wish to salvage and even improve the relationship. Few people enjoy conflict. Generally, the parties wish to prevent further strife. The work-place is an excellent example of an arena in which this mode of conflict resolution is far superior to adversarial position taking.

MEDIATION IN THE WORKPLACE

In the workplace, if a conflict is not resolved amicably, it never ends. Even if a resolution is reached, if it is not mutually satisfying and neglects to address hidden issues, the continuing burden corrupts the relationship. In the work-place, people are profoundly motivated to fully and finally resolve conflict, though they may not have the opportunity or the skills. A mediation program with an established track record will very likely draw voluntarily participation.

The success of mediation is demonstrated by the many schools with peer mediation programs in which students take great pride in their accomplishments. A move toward mediation also can be seen in the court systems nationwide. Lawyers, judges, and litigants are accepting and embracing mediation at an astounding rate. Every state in the country has implemented mediation to some degree and in many states mediation is an integral part of the system.

Of course a mediation program that is new to the workplace will require time and patience. Moving from a grievance culture to a mediation culture is gradual. For most employees, mediation is not part of common experience and participation may be necessary for acceptance. With diligence and a sincere desire, employers and workers can have great success in helping each other to resolve disputes, making the workplace more productive, more satisfying, and generally more pleasant.

Threats to the Mediation Process

Mediation is a remarkably effective and flexible tool for resolving conflict and strengthening relationships. The mediation model is malleable and useful in diverse situations. But it is important to see mediation for what it is—a set of principles and a structural outline. Conceptually, it is a very simple process. It does not have the complex and embedded set of rules that the legal system does. Simplicity and flexibility are part of what makes mediation useful in so many different situations. It is a sound framework for problem solving.

The fact that mediation is so dynamic raises several issues. The first of which may be simply the question, what is mediation? From that, what are the rules that govern the process, what are the boundaries of the structure? When is an interaction mediation and when is it something else? Does simply labeling something mediation make that classification correct? Perhaps these are philosophical questions to be tackled by academics. Or perhaps the nature of mediation is merely a matter of procedure, to be determined by applying rules. On the other hand, perhaps a strict definition of mediation isn't necessary; permission to be flexible is at the heart of the process.

There are certain concepts that define mediation, specific characteristics of a mediator, tools that are regularly used, and procedures that are followed. Although mediation is a distinct process that can be defined, it is not a process that is necessarily constrained by rules. Much of what occurs in mediation is a function of the particular mediator's practice choices and the circumstances of the dispute. Practice theories are now starting to emerge that seek to define the mediation process. Practice theories center around a particular philosophy of problem solving. The mediator's actions are restricted by this philosophy. There are sound arguments for and against adopting a strict mediation protocol. As related disciplines have progressed, more specific practice theories have been created, many of which contradict each other.

In current mediation practice most mediators do not subscribe to a rigid and formalized practice theory. Mediators are more inclined to develop a body of techniques though diverse training and personal experience. Mediators tend to be quite competent at adapting to unique and varied situations. Some issues, however, are of concern to all mediators. Some of these issues involve the interpersonal dynamics between the mediator and the parties. Other concerns relate more to the nature of the process itself; they are more structural matters. Finally, there are philosophical and ideological issues to examine. Because mediation is a relatively young field, the philosophical and ideological underpinnings are only beginning to generate debate.

ISSUES FOR EXAMINATION

There are many situations that occur during mediation that should direct a mediator to review his or her actions. The mediator is constantly making judgments about what is appropriate and effective. Before, during, and after the process, questions arise about why certain interventions work or don't work. A mediator, while impartial, does have influence over the process. The reality of interpersonal dynamics is that when people interact, they have influence over each other. A mediator comes to mediation with an agenda, an idea of the role the players take on and what the process should accomplish. One of the fundamental rules of mediation is that the participants are permitted to make their own choices. But even given this self-determination, the mediator sets limits.

Balance of Power

One concern that impacts a mediator's level of control over the process is the balance of power between the parties. An imbalance of power will make fair and evenhanded negotiations impossible. For instance, in divorce mediation, if one of the parties has been abused, that person may be intimidated into an unfair compromise. Intimidation may manifest itself in various forms. The most obvious way is that the person is simply afraid to be candid for fear of future violence. But a person may respond to intimidation in more subtle ways. Intimidation and fear are not limited to domestic abuse situations and similar responses may occur in any mediation scenario, including the workplace.

While an abusive familial relationship is an obvious example of an imbalance of power, it is possible to identify some imbalance of power in almost every relationship in conflict. An imbalance of power may be obvious or subtle. An imbalance may stem from the dynamics of the personal relationship—some people are simply more assertive than others, for instance. Imbalance may result from business or monetary concerns—for instance, an insurance company may have a great deal of power over a person filing a claim.

Imbalance may be generated from a host of external factors. One example would be a case in which the parties expect to end up in court even though they are attempting mediation. The likelihood of winning or losing a court case can influence the balance of power during negotiations, since winning or losing may not reflect fairness or the wishes of the parties, but instead is dictated by the law.

An imbalance of power inherent in a relationship might contribute to a conflict. Conflicts of all types stem from imbalance of power; here, the conflict derives from pressures of the imbalance. The feelings associated with being dominated by an outside force may generate distrust and hostility, which leads to a battle. The details surrounding the conflict may have nothing to do with the initial cause of the imbalance of power, yet conflict has arisen so the players have something concrete to dispute over, rather than the more intangible sense of "control." This type of power imbalance often occurs between subordinate workers and closely ranked supervisors. It may also be common among coworkers who are vying for attention from supervisors.

Power in the Workplace

The workplace is one of the few arenas where an imbalance of power is intrinsic to the success of the system. In virtually every work situation there are subordinates and superiors. This relationship itself is the catalyst for conflict. There is tremendous pressure in both roles to maintain or gain power. Few work situations exist in which power, image, and control don't affect relationships.

The fact that the workplace is designed to support power imbalances and power struggles should not be construed negatively. It is arguably necessary to the daily function and growth of an organization to maintain a hierarchy of power. Some potential benefits of this structure include:

1. Clear delineation of responsibility and authority.
2. Internal competition that supports personal growth and the desire for success.
3. Vertical movement that positively impacts motivation.
4. The formation of personal and professional alliances through team challenges.
5. Strong alliances and familiarity with competitive environments that support organizational growth through success over rivals.

However, the fact that hierarchy of power and power imbalances are inherent, necessary, and potentially positive in the workplace does not mean this system is without flaws. Even assuming that a rigid organizational structure and the opportunity for growth through competition is largely positive for the workplace, some discontent will arise when relationships are maintained in a less than ideal fashion. The following are some troublesome manifestations of discontent:

1. Upward mobility gained through disabling others, backstabbing.
2. The use of intimidation to gain power.
3. Misplacing blame to save face.
4. Calculated destructive gossip used to weaken competition.

POWER IMBALANCES

In power relationships it is common to interpret an imbalance of power as a show of aggression. One response to dealing with an aggressive relationship is to feel silenced, subservient, or otherwise oppressed. Over time this experience may serve to repress the natural inclination to be open and, when necessary, assertive. It may be difficult for this person to distinguish between safety and danger and make realistic judgements about what the repercussions of their actions might be. In this pattern, a person may find the safest and most comfortable way to behave is to share as little as possible. A person in this position will rarely advocate for his or her needs and wishes.

Expression of needs and wishes is central to the mediation process. This is not to say that open expression will always come easily for the parties, even when there is no seriously destructive relationship between them. One purpose of mediation is for the parties to examine their situation and gain understanding in order to better express their concerns. The extent to which people express themselves will vary greatly according to the personalities of the parties, their relationship, and the nature of the dispute. Different mediations will call for more, or less, intimate expression. Not all mediations are centered around feelings, although feelings always play some part in a conflict. However, there are some situations in which one or both of the parties are so disengaged from their feelings that they are simply unable to express themselves openly. For instance, relationships in which fear and denial result from physical or emotional abuse.

Abuse

Abuse that leads to an imbalance of power can take many forms: physical violence, verbal threats, or intimidation. Conflict by its very nature breeds competition and power, and for those who have the tendency to overwhelm an opponent in order to gain the upper hand, the result may be abuse. Abuse—generally, the use of power to gain control to the detriment of others—occurs in many types of relationships.

The most common form of abuse posing a threat to mediation is domestic violence in divorce cases. Many divorce mediators screen out domestic violence cases and do not permit them to be mediated. Domestic violence is, for the most part, limited to intimate relationships. But it is possible that other types of relationships manifest what might be considered abusive interactions. For instance, sexual harassment or racism in the workplace may be abuse. A domineering boss may be perceived as abusive.

At this time in our culture, the notion of abuse has been expanded to include many forms of undesirable action. With our greater insight into the consequences of emotionally destructive relationships, and the saturation of pop psychology, abusive behaviors have been broadened to include many interactions that do not give rise to physical violence.

What does or does not constitute abuse is generally not for the mediator to decide. Divorce mediators use outside evaluators to determine if there has been abuse. A person who is judging a potential abuse situation lacks the level of neutrality that is required of a mediator. If abuse is determined through an independent screening, some mediators believe the imbalance of power is too great and do not permit these cases to be mediated.

Although the mediator must to some degree protect the parties from unbalanced mediations, granting the mediator the authority to screen out cases causes a variety of problems. First, this affords the mediator great power over other people's problems. One of the fundamental principles of mediation is that the parties are free to make their own decisions. According to mediation philosophy, the mediator is prohibited from deciding which issues should and should not be mediated.

Additionally, screening out any case for mediation may be shortsighted. For instance, some divorce mediators argue that the empowering effects of mediation can shift the power balance. These mediators believe that mediation can be highly effective in situations in which abuse has been present. In mediation the abused party is in a safe environment where they are not only permitted, but required, to demonstrate autonomy, self-determination, and assertiveness. This is an opportunity that is new to the abused partner and will, at least theoretically, change the dynamics in such a way that strength and power shift.

The subject of whether or not mediation is appropriate for relationships in which domestic violence has occurred is instructive. There are some mediators who believe that an imbalance of power resulting from dysfunctional relationships does not preclude productive mediation. In fact, mediation may be a unique opportunity for a disempowered person to assert him or herself in a safe and respectful environment. In mediation the participants are required to listen and respond in a respectful and thoughtful manner. The rules of mediation, in essence, require a balance of power. Therefore, voluntary participation presupposes all abuse will cease.

If it is true that mediation can be an opportunity for the disempowered to interact on a more level playing field, it seems that denying this opportunity would be only a further injustice. The problem is, it is difficult to know who will respond positively and who will not, and, in general, mediators should avoid experimenting at the risk of the parties.

Mediation is a young and growing field and relatively little formalized research has been conducted surrounding these issues. Consequently, there will be dramatically diverse thinking on what constitutes appropriate and effective intervention. Further, opinions are based primarily on theory and anecdotal experience. At this point, individual mediators have the responsibility to decide where to draw lines. The fact that mediation is client-driven will aid the mediator in making distinctions. Mediation is voluntary, participants are never required to engage in any discussion, and mediators are required to respect the participants' wishes.

Manipulation

Imbalance of power may result from behavior more subtle than abuse. Imbalance of power may result when a person behaves in a manipulative fashion, using emotional trickery as a mechanism to obtain what they desire.

Manipulation is a difficult concept to define and may be even more difficult to identify. Manipulation can take many forms. It looks and feels different to different people. It may be fair to say that all behavior is in some way manipulative, even if that manipulation is intended to bring about positive results. For the purpose of this discussion, manipulation has the negative connotation of an action that is intended to bring gain to one at the expense of another.

Because manipulation is such a broad concept and encompasses so many different possible behaviors, accurately and fairly identifying manipulation may be very difficult. An outsider may not be well enough acquainted with the character of a person to recognize manipulation. And an emotionally involved person may misinterpret the intentions of an opponent and identify manipulation where none was intended. It also may be difficult to fairly characterize what is bad or intentional manipulation and what is merely an honest coping mechanism.

From this perspective, it is useful to distinguish manipulation from abuse, and expressions of emotion from manipulation. This can lead to confusion: When is a person displaying honest and healthy emotion, and when is a person attempting to manipulate by using emotion in a calculated fashion? To attempt to answer these questions one must examine emotion and the various ways emotion is expressed and used to maneuver.

EMOTIONAL EXPRESSION IN MEDIATION

Unlike many other organized conflict resolution processes, mediation accepts the notion that emotion is a component in all disputes. Because of this, people may be more freely expressive during mediation than in other meetings where problems are discussed. Genuine displays of emotion are to be expected during mediation. People will show anger, fear, sadness, frustration, hostility, and a host of other feelings that reflect their personal dilemma. Sometimes participants will cry or shout; at times they may swear to highlight a point.

Although mediation is meant to be an opportunity to explore the emotional underpinnings of a problem, it is still a much more formal environment than the home or a therapist's office. While mediation is certainly more casual than a business meeting or courtroom, mediation is not an intimate setting. The mediation process stresses respect and understanding for others' perspectives. It views emotions as a real and important component of problems, but attempts to put these emotions in a rational context.

Venting emotion is perfectly acceptable during mediation. It is both a release and a useful way to share information. When another person witnesses an emotional expression, it is an invaluable clue into what is feeding the disagreement and often reflects issues that have not been previously discussed. At the same time, mediation is not group therapy. Participants are not at liberty to express emotion in such a dramatic way that there is a negative cost to the process or other participants. Mediation is designed to be an informal, yet professional, meeting. Because mediation supports a meeting of the minds, but does not advocate unrestrained freedom of expression, emotional expressions are usually displayed in a controlled manner.

Mediation can be therapeutic, but it is not therapy. And in many cases the people involved in the dispute are not intimate friends. In most circumstances the parties will not think it is appropriate to display their heightened emotions in a way that will make them vulnerable and make others uncomfortable. While it is common to see some tears or hear a raised voice, it is not common for a person to break down sobbing or for a violent shouting match to occur. Although some conflicts are more emotionally charged than others, and expressions of feeling will vary, for the most part, the participants in mediation display what might be considered socially appropriate behavior.

Mediator Responses to Emotion

Although it is not the mediator's role to control the emotional expressions of the parties, the mediator does play a part in the direction that the mediation takes. From this perspective, the mediator might encourage expression of emotion though prompts that indicate showing feeling is acceptable. The mediator might demonstrate empathy if a person begins to cry; a mediator should feel free to show concern for the participants' feelings. While demonstrating concern, a mediator can still remain impartial, appreciating how a person feels does not constitute agreeing with their position. It is important for a mediator to clearly identify that empathy is not tantamount to taking sides.

It is within the mediator's responsibility to have a heightened awareness of the dynamics between the parties and the individual behavior of each person. This includes being sensitive to emotions, both those overtly displayed and more subtle. While most of the time people will be hesitant to show dramatic emotional responses, this does not minimize the power that even more subtle expressions of emotions have on other people. Particularly in a context in which emotionality is not expected, emotional displays cannot be disregarded.

Extreme Emotion

Most people have some awareness that behaving in an emotional way can be a very useful tool that has a strong impact on other people. This is not to suggest that people commonly resort to false emotion with the explicit intent to manipulate. But even genuine heartfelt emotion can be used as a tool to influence, and this influence may or may not be calculated.

It is certainly conceivable that rather than restraining emotions during mediation, a person might exaggerate their emotions as a way to get attention and sympathy. This may be an intentional ploy to manipulate, or an innocent and unconscious response to a stressful situation. Either way, intense emotion can be a stumbling block to mediation. Although expressing emotion is encouraged during mediation, extremely intense emotional outbursts can be distracting to all the people involved.

It is very difficult to focus on anything else when a person is highly agitated. When someone is upset, the conversation naturally turns to that person. The focus is placed on the cause of those feelings and what can be done to soothe the pain. Although this may be a necessary and very useful experience during mediation, it can be highly distracting to the process when these feelings become the primary topic of conversation. Focusing on extreme emotion requires complete attention. Everyone present is expected to demonstrate concern for the emotionally injured person. In this circumstance the non-emotional party is thwarted from sharing his or her own thoughts, it may appear callous to assert contradictory feelings or a different perspective.

Role of the Mediator. Extreme emotion also presents a number of problems for the mediator, who as a coordinator helps to direct the conversation. After an initial expression of empathy by the mediator and an attempt to discuss and clarify the feelings being expressed, it is incumbent on the mediator to redirect the discussion away from the emotional issue. This can be a risky undertaking and requires a great deal of sensitivity and skill. The mediator does not want to appear rude and insensitive; when a person is in a highly emotional state, craving attention, he or she may not be in a position to appreciate the predicament of the mediator. If by redirecting the focus away from the emotional person, the mediator seems to negate the significance of the emotions being expressed, trust in the mediator may be reduced.

Genuine Emotion

If a person is expressing a genuine outburst of emotion, this expression is an important and often very productive process; people can learn a great deal from their own and other people's emotional responses. In this case, the mediator may not wish to redirect the discussion away from the emotion, and instead focus on the emotion in an attempt to learn from it. This should not become therapy, but rather a focused exploration of how these feelings are impacting on the problem. With genuine emotion, in whatever form—anger, sadness, or frustration—the intense response escalates and then de-escalates to the point at which a person is then able to reflect. The mediator and the parties should then reach a point where more rational, or at least calm, discussion is possible. Most emotion expressed during mediation reflects pent-up frustration rather than deep trauma.

Calculated Emotion

A problem may arise if an emotional display is more calculated than spontaneous, or underlying the expression reflects a need to create drama in order to gain sympathy and attention. It is more difficult to adequately respond to emotion that is calculated or put on. One reason for this is that there is no natural progression of the behavior. With a dramatic emotion, a natural de-escalation does not always occur. Emotion of this type may be employed to manipulate. It is more a calculated aggressive response, and it is difficult to predict the progression of these emotional displays.

Another difficulty for the mediator is that calculated emotion serves a purpose different from more genuine feelings. Heartfelt emotion is a release, and often shows an insight into a problem. It is informative for both sides and can lead to a productive discussion and a greater sense of empathy and understanding. Calculated emotion serves a separate purpose. Although it also generates sympathy, it draws attention to the emotional person in a way that may be distracting to the discussion. Since the feelings expressed are not a real reflection of elements that feed into the problem, there can be no insight into how to resolve the problem. At most, there will be insight into how that person responds to conflict. This display will be a clue as to what to expect from that person throughout the resolution process and into the future.

An added concern is that very often calculated emotion is not really a deliberate ploy, but rather an unconscious pattern of behavior common to that person's experience. For whatever reason, that person uses emotion as a tool to get what they want and need. And frankly, most people do this to some degree in their lives, precisely because it is so effective. Because of this, it may be very difficult to distinguish between true and calculated emotion, even for the person expressing it.

Lack of Expression. To complicate matters, calculated emotion may take the form of no expression of emotion at all. There is immense power in refusing, or being unable, to express feelings. It is blinding to those trying to communicate with the nonemotive person. Working under the assumption that all conflict has an emotional element, a lack of emotional expression creates a void in understanding the conflict. Rather than sympathy, there is a lack of a connectedness that alienates others. Without a personal connection, which is often found through a mutual understanding of feelings, it is difficult to come to some meeting of the minds on a problem, particularly if one person is openly emotional and one is closed.

This is a common, even stereotypical, dilemma between women and men, and causes a great deal of confusion in relationships. As a generalization, men are sometimes overwhelmed by a woman's dramatic expression of emotion, and women are equally overwhelmed by a man's lack of expression. This makes connection difficult. Of course this predicament is not only confined to men and women, but it is a recognizable scenario in many relationships.

In-House Workplace Mediation

It is undeniable that work conflict can be a serious and confounding problem. With this realization, most organizations have procedures that attempt to address employee conflict or grievances. Less serious problems are usually dealt with in an informal manner, through immediate supervisors. But dealing with conflict, even in an informal setting, can be quite intimidating.

For most people, their job represents more than a livelihood, and issues of self-worth and pride are involved. For this reason, when conflict arises, and job performance or work behavior is scrutinized, people sense a threat to their professional and personal status. Even if the threat is not serious, defenses flair. But conflict affects others in a work circle as well. A complaint against one person may impact the superiors and subordinates of that person. It also affects the person who made the complaint. In many work environments lodging a complaint against a fellow worker is taboo and people will avoid expressing their concerns until the situation reaches a crisis level. Conflict on the job forces people to address the frightening unknown and disrupts equilibrium in work relationships.

THE GRIEVANCE PROCESS

Formal grievance processes, the typical method for handling work conflict, are usually designed to handle problems that have reached a critical stage. Grievance processes are generally structured to promote the organization's needs rather than the worker's individual or personal needs. Grievance procedures can be cumbersome, confusing, inflexible, and intimidating. They also may be designed to discourage participation. This is logical from the traditional perspective that holds that interpersonal conflict is a private matter. Grievance processes are traditionally designed to handle strictly work-related matters rather than interpersonal conflict, which is thought to only incidentally affect work.

Most organizations do not want employees to use the grievance process unless absolutely necessary. To do so distracts all the workers who are involved in the dispute. Working through a grievance requires time, effort, and funds that could be employed otherwise. To discourage its use, the grievance process is often made difficult, thus employees are thwarted and refrain from filing formal complaints. Perhaps also to deter participation, or because the processes are rarely used, many formal grievance procedures are poorly organized and are not efficient at dispensing just results. Neglecting to address the flaws in grievance procedures is shortsighted since an inefficient process can actually serve to increase job strife.

EMPLOYEE RELATIONSHIPS

Employee dissatisfaction on the job is often progressive, escalating over time. Frequently, annoyances or frustrations are overlooked when they occur, but they are not forgotten. Problems, both big and small, are kept hidden if employees feel uncomfortable or unjustified when disclosing their concerns. The workplace does not tend to be an environment in which people look favorably on open dialogue about interpersonal matters, or issues that are perceived as minor. In our society there is an unspoken, yet clear, distinction between appropriate home behavior and work behavior. Open expression is seen as healthy with friends and family, while at work, people are bombarded with messages about teamwork, which implies disregarding annoyances. This perception of appropriate work behavior makes expressing disapproval on the job seem childish, unprofessional, and disruptive.

This view overlooks the reality that work relationships are intimate and personal. People spend a great deal of time with each other at the workplace. Bonds and friendships are formed. Hostilities and frustrations grow. To add to this mix, there are both clear-cut and hidden power relationships at work, as there often are at home. At home or at work, people bring with them their individual personalities, their private troubles, and their interpersonal strengths and weaknesses. It is naive and potentially destructive to disregard the complexities of work relationships. Complications and conflict will inevitably arise when people work together. It is more productive to understand these issues and address them forthrightly, rather than to disregard them until problems escalate.

It is not necessarily any easier to calm and settle disputes at a work setting than in other areas of life. Many people will avoid conflict until they feel there are no productive alternatives. Conflict is confusing, disruptive, frightening, and can be emotionally and professionally destructive. However, one of the benefits of the workplace setting for resolving conflict is that a formal process can be instituted whereby people are encouraged to deal with conflict before it becomes overwhelmingly disruptive. With forethought and planning, the employer can do for the workplace what many cannot do for their homes— design a concrete conflict resolution approach that is clear, functional, and accessible. The employer can also create an environment in which people trust the process and want to participate, where people recognize that there is more satisfaction in resolving disputes early, rather than waiting until the problem escalates and becomes overwhelming.

IMPACT OF A GRIEVANCE

Workplace disputes can be very difficult to resolve amicably. To bring forth a grievance is risky in many respects. First, it may put another's reputation, or even their job, in jeopardy. Whether real or only perceived, the threat of a grievance is a serious emotional blow. A grievance carries an implication that the supervisor has managed ineffectively. Because this superior is in a position of authority, a grievance is a threat to that authority. Finally, a certain amount of culpability may be attributed to the employer, who is ultimately responsible for a stable work environment. Even if the employer is not directly responsible for the conflict, failure to maintain a stable work environment through adequate policies and supervision suggests a flaw in management.

Since filing a grievance has serious implications, many employees may only feel free to complain about work problems in an informal manner. Generally, an employee does not make a formal complaint until a problem appears overwhelming or out of control. At that point, from the employee's perspective, the protections set up by the employer have failed. As a result, a sense of distrust has developed. That distrust is frequently transferred to the dispute resolution process itself, making the process more difficult and reducing the likelihood of satisfactory long-term resolution.

To a supervisor, grievances often appear frivolous, unfounded, or motivated by some hidden agenda. Since it is the supervisor's responsibility to oversee immediate subordinates, to be cognizant of the work environment and the dynamics of interpersonal interaction, a supervisor will often be aware of brewing trouble. When a grievance is filed, it suggests that the supervisor has disregarded the problem or did not intervene effectively. Whether the supervisor was aware of the problem and did not act, or was simply unaware of the problem, when subordinates notify the employer of a problem and request outside assistance, the supervisor is held responsible. Partly in self-defense, supervisors may attribute a grievance to overreaction.

As a defensive measure, the supervisor will respond with some explanation for their own inaction. This explanation may or may not be justified. There certainly may be legitimate reasons that the supervisor did not know, failed to act, or failed to finally resolve a conflict. But from both the subordinate employee's perspective, and the employer's perspective, the supervisor has failed. Whether justified or unjustified, the supervisor must vindicate himself, which further taints the dispute resolution process, making trust and open communication more difficult.

As a result of the grievance, the employer is apt to question both the complaining employee and the supervisor. The highest concern is that the organization is run smoothly and productively. Any conflict, particularly a formal grievance, causes discord that is potentially disruptive to the entire workforce. Serious complaints are rarely heard in a vacuum. Other employees will know and discuss the issues freely.

A formal grievance is always a threat. There is the real potential of disrupted productivity and morale, the escalation of conflict that spurs other workers to complain, terminations, and possible legal action. Employers will often take dramatic steps to prevent widespread disruption, even if that action is not justified. Employer overreaction hinders productive short-term and long-term conflict resolution. Where there is fear about a process, there is little faith or trust in the process.

In sum, assumptions are made about any worker who files a formal grievance. Grievances are seen as either justified or frivolous. Both assumptions have serious ramifications. Grievances follow dissatisfaction with work or personal behavior. These complaints are invariably taken as a personal affront, which results in damaged egos and devastated relationships. Dissatisfaction has a tendency to escalate with time. For example, disapproval that is first directed at a worker becomes a grievance filed against a supervisor; frustration and disappointment finally lead to a termination and then a lawsuit filed against the organization.

OUTLETS FOR CONFLICT

We live in a society in which we enjoy personal freedoms, independence, and inalienable rights. Perhaps because of our many entitlements, feelings of worth and personal satisfaction seem to be essential to maintain a productive workforce. In other words, happy workers make better workers. Happy workers make consistent workers who stay on the job, curtailing constant retraining. Happy workers are also more likely to accept the flaws in the organization, such as low wages and long working hours. In short, happy workers don't quit their jobs, don't employ labor union processes, and don't file lawsuits. Without a working outlet for grievances workers cannot be happy. Serious consequences follow.

This may appear to be a simplistic summary of such complex subjects as worker motivation, job satisfaction, and interpersonal conflict. And frankly it is. If the goal is to understand exactly why people behave in a certain way, the foregoing explanations will not suffice. But in examining the primary issue at hand—how to resolve conflict in efficient and satisfying ways—the fundamental truths are as follows:

1. Conflict exists in the workplace.
2. Conflict is destructive on a personal and economic level.
3. Employers must implement strategies to address conflict that are practical, effective, efficient, and trustworthy.

The people responsible for a workplace mediation program are generally not interested in spending enormous amounts of time studying complex issues. All people acknowledge that disputes exist. For the most part, both workers and employers would prefer amicable solutions that do not end in the loss of jobs or lawsuits. Employers and employees are on a continuing quest, not necessarily to find absolute answers, but to find tools that work. So the question remains: what works?

Lawsuits

Since all disputes at work have the potential to lead to formal grievances with serious consequences, grievances that are not settled amicably and in a timely fashion do often lead to lawsuits. It is possible to divide workplace disputes into two general categories. First are the scenarios in which a serious violation occurred. Examples of this might be drug use on the job, violence causing physical harm, or grievous sexual harassment. In these cases, filing a lawsuit may be a rational and even necessary step to assure a just result.

The second category includes more common offenses that occur in the workplace. Examples of these might be interpersonal conflict, disagreements about work assignments, pay and benefit issues, and job performance concerns. These types of issues often begin with small frustrations, but, over time, when not properly addressed, can become all-consuming.

Not only does work suffer when employees experience an overwhelming frustration, the gravity of the problem seems to mushroom. These conflicts often take on an importance disproportionate to the nature of the problem, which could be easily solved if appropriate steps were taken. It is these cases that end up at a lawyer's door and become a huge burden to employees and employers alike.

Sometimes issues such as these become lawsuits, brought merely as a threat. The motivation for such a drastic measure depends greatly on the person and the circumstances. One common rationale for initiating a threatening lawsuit is the sense that a lawsuit is the only way to be heard. A typical reason employees take drastic measures against employers is simply to make a point. When a person feels disregarded, unimportant, belittled, or marginalized, a lawsuit is a proactive way to be taken seriously. Unfortunately, in the effort to make a point, all the people involved are forced to expend tremendous amounts of money, time, and emotional energy. Even the winner of such a lawsuit pays dearly, financially, professionally, and personally.

Labor Unions

The organized labor movement has attempted to rectify problems by bringing in third party advocates, as well as insisting on extensive rules for worker protection. Whether or not one agrees with labor union philosophy, several things are clear. First, organized labor has made great strides for worker protection and dramatically changed the way our society perceives worker rights and employer responsibilities. Yet even with these strides, few workers have real employment security. And, second, at this time, the majority of workers and employers do not wish to engage in the organized labor process.

Grievance Processes

Most workplace grievance procedures use one of three typical designs. A common design for smaller or traditional employers is a grievance procedure that permits people to present their complaint at several supervision levels, moving up the ranks through the hierarchy of supervision. The grievance ultimately ends with a high-level administrator making a final determination.

Another type of grievance procedure, often used interdepartmentally within large or public organizations, involves a panel of decision makers. The panel is composed of members who hold various positions within the hierarchy of the organization, to promote objective decision making.

A third and less common grievance procedure is utilized by some government-funded organizations. This procedure offers statutory remedies through a "grievance board." Here, determinations are made after a formal hearing by an objective outsider, such as an administrative law judge.

The actual and perceived objectivity of each of these procedures is limited. It may be difficult for a decision maker to maintain total objectivity when he or she is employed by one of the disputing sides. Alternatively, a disputant may believe the decision maker is not objective, thus hindering progress. Any time decisions are made within a community it must be assumed that there are risks to participation. Prejudice comes in many forms, sometimes as subjectivity resulting from conscious decision making and other times as unintended consequence of a system.

Each of the above grievance procedures has another potentially destructive common element. The underlying premise is adversarial. One side attempts to prove that an error occurred; the other side attempts to prove that it did not. It is inherent in the process that each side take a position and advocate zealously. Any concession is perceived as an admission of weakness. Even if a concession does not destroy one's case altogether, it may foster the impression that the case is weaker than claimed.

Mediation

Mediation is not based on the adversarial model. It is structured to resolve the dispute according to the specific needs and desires of the people involved. Mediation is about collaboration and compromise. Mediation permits the disputing parties to make their own evaluations and determinations. The impartial third party mediator has no authority to judge. Mediation is an opportunity for the participants to analyze conflict. During the mediation, patterns of behavior are examined. As a result, the participants gain an understanding of the cause and effect of disputes. Decisions made during mediation are accepted as the best solution to the problem.

It is essential to realize that although mediation is about fairness, it is not necessarily about justice. If the underlying motivation for a grievance is the principle, mediation may not be appropriate. Mediation cannot change laws, in a legal sense it cannot punish, and it is not a substitute for legal protection when behavior has crossed into the realm of immoral, unethical, or criminal.

Mediation can be used in-house at a workplace as part of a grievance procedure or conflict resolution process. Mediation has proven to be an effective alternative to the legal dispute resolution system for many years and is growing dramatically in use and acceptance. It is certainly possible to adopt the philosophy and process of mediation for in-house employment disputes. However, some creativity and flexibility are necessary to avoid repeating the common pitfalls of other grievance procedures.

Requirements. An employer must be committed to the success of a mediation process. The mediation process must be designed with integrity and objectivity. Any notion that mediation is merely a seemingly fair way to reprimand must be totally dismissed. Many employers feel very strongly about maintaining power over their workers. If this is the case, mediation is not the appropriate dispute resolution tool. If a sham mediation system is implemented, one in which the autonomy of the participants is illusory, the resulting distrust will likely destroy relationships rather than bolster them.

The employer and the participants must accept that all mediation discussions are private and confidential; notes taken during mediation will never be included in a personnel file. It is imperative that the participants feel free to speak openly without any fear of embarrassment or reprimand. The employer must ensure that there will be absolutely no retribution for using the mediation process; this is accomplished through a comprehensive set of rules and procedures that are strictly enforced.

In addition to the employer's commitment, the employees must be equally willing to participate openly and honorably; this requires a sincere desire for fair resolution and trust in the employer. It also requires putting anger aside and dismissing any notions of revenge. Mediation cannot be used to undermine or disrupt the workplace, punish coworkers, or avoid responsibilities.

Challenges. At the outset of any in-house mediation program there is one immense battle to tackle. For many complicated reasons, some of which are inherent in hierarchical relationships and some of which are specific to an individual workplace, there is often a serious lack of trust pervasive in the work environment. Perhaps management doesn't trust the staff and at the same time the staff doesn't trust management. This leads to hostility and an overactive grapevine. Lack of trust can be pervasive and take many destructive forms.

Mediation is one very useful tool for building trust in an organization, while at the same time mediation is not very effective without the existence of trust. There is no easy escape from this dilemma. Mediation is one tool available to build trust and make a workplace happier. Any change requires examination, dedication, proaction, and time. Often, the first step toward making change has the biggest impact. When employees are aware of management's willingness to change, an immediate and complete transformation is not necessary to make the work environment less conflictual and more satisfying.

Professional versus Peer Mediation

When any workplace designs a mediation program, it will be faced with the question of whether to hire outside professional mediators or to use staff as peer mediators. It is difficult to predict which type of mediation program will be more effective for any given institution. But peer mediation and professional mediation programs offer very different benefits and also have varying costs in terms of time and money. An organization should consider the pros and cons of both options before committing time and resources.

PROFESSIONAL MEDIATORS

The obvious benefit of hiring professional mediators is their expertise. If the goal is to settle a small number of serious cases as efficiently as possible, and the employer is willing to pay a premium for services, a professional mediator may be most appropriate. Professional mediators will also be effective in assisting organizations with more general goals, such as strengthening communication and decreasing hostility in the workplace. A downside of hiring professionals is the cost. Professional mediators usually charge by the hour. However, although their fees can be high, a few hours of mediation is certainly less expensive than a complicated lawsuit. Mediation also saves money lost to downtime that can result from a continuing dispute. Many organizations hire professional mediators on a consultant basis with great success.

Because there is no fee regulation for professional workplace mediators, prices will vary. As rule of thumb, an organization should expect to pay the going rate for that mediator's base profession. For example, if the mediator is licensed as a lawyer, expect to pay the hourly rate of a lawyer; the same would hold for social workers, psychologists, and so on. If the organization does not foresee using mediation on a regular basis, or the primary interest is in taking an aggressive step toward preventing lawsuits, hiring a professional mediator might ultimately be less expensive than training staff as peer mediators, who will not be highly skilled immediately.

PEER MEDIATORS

Alternatively, implementing a peer mediation program may benefit an organization in ways that hiring outside mediators could not. If the goal is partly to change the climate of an organization, teach better interpersonal skills, and support the notion that the employees can help themselves, peer mediation has great potential. In the past, peer mediation has most often been used in schools or in communities, where the goals are broader than those of settling arguments and preventing lawsuits.

With young people, peer mediation is used to enhance overall conflict resolution skills and critical thinking, and to strengthen long-term relationships. Peers in the schools or the workplace have a personal and intimate understanding of underlying attitudes, systematic problems, cultural norms, and social expectations of their own communities. Peers are already familiar with the types of problems that typically arise and may have great insight into why they occur. This connection leads to a potentially strong trust relationship between the mediator and the parties.

The same circumstance would be true in communities in which friends and neighbors are helping each other with a shared goal. Community mediation has also proven very successful, despite the fact that the mediators are not professionally trained. The unity of coming together to work though long-standing issues can be powerful. To coin a phrase, the participants "take ownership" of the problem. When people work as a group and acknowledge the harm that conflict can cause, resolving problems independently fosters pride and satisfaction. People become empowered as they learn to take control of issues that once seemed out of control. This is as true in the workplace as in the neighborhood.

CHOOSING

Despite the substantive arguments for using one form of mediation over another, decisions are always impacted by financial considerations. Many organizations simply cannot afford to pay hundreds of dollars to settle a small dispute. If the purpose of implementing a workplace mediation program is in part to resolve small problems before they escalate, than virtually every problem is a candidate for mediation. If this is the case, hiring a mediator to work through issues that initially appear inconsequential may seem absurd. But enlisting peers to help dissipate that same argument before it becomes highly disruptive makes a great deal of sense.

It is also important to consider other factors in predicting the cost of a mediation program. For most organizations mediation will be new and unfamiliar; the philosophy of mediation is quite different from that of traditional grievance processes. Any large-scale procedural change in an organization, particularly one that claims to change a cultural environment, requires time and effort before it is wholly accepted. The workforce requires education about the process; trust must be built between workers and management.

The most logical way to begin an education process is with training sessions coupled with public relations efforts. And whether the mediation program employs professional mediators or peer mediators, these educational efforts are necessary. Education will serve even those workers who will never act as mediators. All people benefit from training in the philosophy and techniques of mediation. For a workplace that plans to shift from a grievance culture to a mediation culture, using either professional or peer mediators, an understanding of the process is essential for acceptance. These initial trainings are also a useful way to identify those people who would make competent, thoughtful, and interested peer mediators. Those selected then go on to more comprehensive training if a peer mediation program is to be implemented. Even if an organization plans to hire professional mediators, some time and money should be invested in educating the workforce.

One of the primary benefits of mediation over other grievance procedures is its effectiveness for resolving low-level disputes prior to the critical stage. For this reason it may be most productive to design a program in which mediation is available for any conflict, regardless of whether the issues appear inconsequential to outsiders. Professional mediation may be impractical for this sort of program. Mediation is also excellent for heightening productive communication, building conflict resolution skills, and strengthening interpersonal relationships. The availability of mediation to the workforce impacts the extent to which these additional rewards are reaped.

In a cost/benefit analysis an organization might find that the most productive and cost-effective measure is to implement a peer mediation program. The option of hiring a professional if a particular case mandates is always open. In a situation in which the dispute is so dire or complex that a professional is required, the money allotted to professional mediation will be well spent. In dramatic circumstances, the cost of hiring a mediator will still be far less than investing in a lawsuit. In the long run, whichever mediation program is implemented, the benefits of mediation far outweigh the costs.

The Legal System

Although this book is not primarily concerned with mediation in the legal system, it is useful to explore the use of mediation in this arena. Mediation is actively employed in court systems around the country. Nationwide, there is a good deal of mediation occurring in the family court system to resolve divorce and child custody issues. Many civil courts also sponsor mediation to unburden the court dockets and offer an alternative to the adversarial system. Lawyers, judges, therapists, social workers, and other professionals affiliated with the legal system are becoming convinced that mediation is a productive, affordable, and humane way to resolve disputes.

The legal system is certainly not the only area in which mediation is becoming popular, but it is an arena in which practitioners have a good deal of experience and knowledge to share. Most law schools now offer courses in mediation and alternative dispute resolution, and other departments at colleges and universities are following suit. There are many reasons why the legal system is among the most active in promoting the progression of mediation. There is money available for experimental programs in the legal system. But, more significantly, the legal system is the most complex and advanced formal bureaucracy solely relegated to resolving conflict.

Although therapists, counselors, teachers, and other helping professionals do assist people in resolving their disputes, conflict resolution is just one of the goals of these practitioners. The legal system is therefore a logical and important proving ground for mediation programs and should be referenced when discussing other mediation applications, particularly if there is any possibility that disputes will be referred to the courts.

LEGAL SETTLEMENT

Many people believe that virtually every legal case that is filed, or every lawsuit, progresses to litigation. The truth is that almost all legal cases never reach a courtroom. They are settled by the parties in conjunction with their lawyers well before a trial is held. In fact, it is assumed in legal circles that approximately 95 percent of all law cases are settled without ever going to court. The process of legal settlement occurs when lawyers from opposing sides engage in negotiations that involve bargaining for acceptable losses. Settlement is a compromise. Mediation is to some degree an outgrowth of legal bargaining and negotiation. Much can be learned about mediation from examining legal settlement.

The fact that most cases settle before a trial is instructive for a mediator. Legal settlement suggests the following concepts:

1. In filing a legal claim, people do not expect to ultimately get everything they want. They understand that there will be compromise.

2. In settling a claim, people will accept less than they really want. People are willing to compromise.

3. In coming to a compromise, people expect to receive less then they initially request. They understand that a compromise requires accepting less than initially asked for.

4. In filing a claim it can be assumed that most people request more than they actually want or believe they are entitled to. In anticipating compromise, people exaggerate their demands. In this regard, the process of bargaining involves a certain amount of dishonesty, or at least misrepresentation. Disdainfully referred to as posturing, the positions taken when filing lawsuits are not entirely true representations of what people expect and are willing to receive. It can be extrapolated from this that, when filing claims, people sometimes ask for more than they deserve.

THE NATURE OF NEGOTIATIONS

Although these observations are linked to filing legal claims, similar positions are also taken when attempting to resolve disputes outside the legal system. Bargaining, negotiation, and compromise are a common feature of most of our lives. People bargain with employers, coworkers, spouses, family, and children. A fundamental part of all relationships is bargaining and compromise. Although legal bargaining and mediation are more formal or structured forms of bargaining, many of the same tools and strategies are used when engaging in a business negotiation or an interpersonal negotiation.

The art of legal negotiations may seem complex, but the process of legal bargaining can be compared to a haggling process, such as negotiating at a flea market. A buyer sees something that he wants and asks the seller the price. Negotiations begin. The seller asks $5.00 for the item. The buyer says, "I won't pay a penny more than $2.00." The seller asks for $4.50. The buyer comes back with $2.50, and so on. While this is a simplification of any legal negotiation, the fundamental interaction is the same.

Both sides begin negotiations from exaggerated positions. Both are perceived positions of power. The seller knows the buyer wants to buy—that gives the seller power. The buyer knows the seller wants to sell—that gives the buyer power. Negotiations continue until the power balance is just slightly uneven. Either the seller concedes at the point he thinks the buyer will walk away or the buyer concedes at the point where she fears the seller will sell to someone else. Both sides know the bargaining is dishonest and no one knows exactly when the balance point will be reached. In secret, both sides have a bottom line. For instance, the buyer will never spend more than $3.00 and the seller will never take less than $3.00. If negotiations continue and bottom lines are met, a successful negotiation transpires.

BOUNDARIES OF THE LAW

While the basic structure of negotiation is similar regardless of the subject matter, there are elements that make legal negotiations unique and far more complex. The differences of legal negotiations highlight circumstances in which resolving issues through legal channels is more appropriate than mediation. The legal system consists of a complex set of formal rules and procedures that does not exist anywhere else in society. There are times when the nature of the dispute requires that precedents and strict guidelines for behavior be applied to assure fair play and justice. There are situations in which individuals cannot or should not manage their own dispute.

In the legal system, while all issues are subject to debate and critique, the law creates clear and strong boundaries. The boundaries the law sets establish limited starting and ending points for every problem. The law predetermines fairness and in doing so regulates the steps that are required to reach a final resolution. Because of this structure, participants in the legal system can make well-informed predictions about the potential outcome of the dispute before becoming deeply entrenched in the process. The law also establishes predetermined power relationships in an attempt to thwart the abuse of power, applied in an arbitrary manner.

For success in planning the course of a lawsuit and accurately predicting the outcome, attorneys are used by the disputants. The primary reason people seek the assistance of legal counsel is so they can be guided and informed. Lawyers design and initiate the resolution process and make calculated decisions based on the results they wish to achieve. Unlike other forms of dispute resolution, including mediation, the law structures problem solving so that the process can be preplanned with an organized strategy. Law aims to filter out the unpredictable and uncontrollable nature of disputes, namely the emotional element.

The Example of Divorce

Divorce is one of the most emotionally charged events people experience. It is difficult for divorcing couples to make rational decisions when feeling frustration and pain. To counter the potential injustices that may result from decisions based on extreme feelings, the law creates boundaries that overrule emotion. For instance, many states now mandate an equal distribution of marital property upon divorce. The sides can argue about who gets the car versus the house, but, in the end, the division must be equal. These boundaries exclude emotions and personal desires from the decision-making process and protect those who have less power. These boundaries also make it possible for a lawyer to inform his or her client about what to expect from the process.

An even more volatile issue is child custody. It seems it would be difficult to regulate such a uniquely personal problem, for situations vary greatly. But the potential for personal devastation and harm to innocent children is so great that precedents and rules have been designed to set legal boundaries. The parties are required to temper their feelings and actions to abide by these rules. Because of the rules, people are aware when they breach the code of behavior deemed acceptable by society. Additionally, each party has guidance as to what to expect from an opponent.

In the case of child custody, historical legal precedents favor the mother. More modern precedents have set rules regarding parental fitness, discrimination, and the best interest of the child. Using these precedents as guides, the parties can plan how to address the problem, they are informed about potential obstacles, and have a reference for becoming emotionally prepared. When a person knows what to expect it is often much easier to deal with the problem.

Boundaries and Justice

The boundaries the law sets are very important. The law helps to maintain a civilized society, a goal certainly out of reach if individuals are permitted to act solely in accord with their emotional responses. In many instances, justice, or the socially fair resolution of disputes, can only be served through the legal system, a system that defines collective notions of right and wrong. A system that, at its best, elevates the weak to an even playing field with the strong.

As a society we have made great advances through the use of the legal process. For instance, laws and lawsuits protect against racial and sexual discrimination. Through civil rights laws there is an attempt to control unequal treatment based on race and gender. People who believe they have been discriminated against have a forum that permits judgment based on objective standards. Laws protect against dangerous products and environmental hazards. Laws also make the home and workplace safer with rules that prohibit unsafe products and working conditions. This prevents wealthy and powerful individuals from becoming more wealthy at the expense of the general public. Laws that protect people and property create standards for behavior and consequences for a breach of those standards, including money damages for people who have been injured and cannot be healed in other ways.

Our legal system is not flawless and many argue over the appropriate boundaries that the law should set. However, over time, with continuous evaluation and reformation, the legal system continues to advance the social and physical health of the citizens it aims to protect.

WEAKNESSES IN THE SYSTEM

There is no question that a complex legal system is necessary for the maintenance of a functioning, progressive, civil society. But this does not mean that the legal system should be the sole mechanism for the resolution of all conflicts. There are some problems that are best resolved by other means. There are some features of interpersonal conflict, particularly emotional issues, that the legal system is not designed to address.

The legal system can also be expensive, inefficient, stressful, and may not present the same options for the wealthy and the poor. In addition, the legal system removes the individual from his or her predicaments. The system usurps problems and addresses them in a fashion that is most conducive to the ongoing management of the system. It often ignores the individual needs of the people involved.

The legal system is rigid. It does not reflect individual needs, but rather societal needs. Although this is a logical way to address large-scale issues and protect masses of people, it is not necessarily a logical way to bring individual people together and prevent future conflict. The law binds creativity in decision making. It hinders the judges and juries from finding fitting solutions to unique problems. Because the rules of the system are so restrictive, judgments that do not fit within strict protocol put the credibility of the decision maker in question. Unorthodox decisions are often overruled further along in the system. Law aims at protecting society as a whole, but ignores the individual.

The legal system separates people from their personal responsibility. A dispute turned over to a lawyer becomes the lawyer's case. The client has little say in strategy decisions and is not required to examine the underlying issues of the dispute. Within the legal system, even when a case is resolved, the factors that initially caused the problem often remain. In addition, the legal system assumes that a day in court is sufficient to satisfy the parties, quelling anger, frustration, humiliation, and other emotional pain associated with the dispute. While the legal process does offer a sense of closure and relief for some people, it is at the cost of autonomy in decision making and the relationships of the people involved in the dispute.

Lawsuits do force people to resolve issues, but rarely do people come together at the completion of a lawsuit sharing a sense of satisfaction and mutual understanding. The legal system perpetuates hostility. It promotes the notion that our opponents are our enemies. Certainly this is the best route in some circumstances, but many problems can and should be resolved by adopting a nonadversarial solution strategy.

Finally, the legal system is costly and time-consuming. Even if a person has the financial resources to effectively utilize the system, the prolonged process often exacerbates the dispute and permanently destroys relationships. To assure all the protections demanded in society—constitutional rights, for instance—a system has been created that requires enormous amounts of knowledge, time, and paperwork. Legal motions, hearings, briefs, and all the trappings of the system demand complete commitment to the process, regardless of the costs.

While not suggesting that any portion of the process be compromised, there may be times when it is unnecessary to engage in these extensive requirements to amicably and justly resolve a problem. Since it would be unwise to weaken the necessary protections within the system, it makes sense to create a separate system that offers alternatives.

Recognizing Alternatives

It is argued that the legal system has become overwhelmingly pervasive in everyday life. The legal process is promoted and idealized in the popular culture of movies and television. Frequently when a problem arises, the first line of defense is to arm with the protection of a lawyer. Rather than focusing on resolving the problem and reclaiming a sense of well-being, a dispute is seen as an opportunity for personal gain. While the legal system does serve an essential purpose, it does not cure all societal ills. In fact, sometimes it does more harm than good. The legal system weakens relationships, neglects emotional issues, and does little to deter repeating destructive patterns.

There are good reasons for handing over some disputes to an outsider, to have an objective system resolve highly complex or destructive problems. However, alternatives can also be created that support personal responsibility and empower the people in conflict, strengthening relationships for the future.

Part Two

The Mediation Process

The Mediation Process

Mediation is more than a technique used for resolving conflict; it reflects a particular philosophy of the world and of interpersonal relationships. Mediation includes an ideology. Mediation embraces the concepts of empathy, compromise, and acceptance. Mediation acknowledges that different perspectives occur that are inherently valid and purposeful; that conflict exists for a reason and the resolution of conflict is always important, a regeneration in the cycle of life.

Mediation also espouses a respect for people: that, given the opportunity, people are competent and able to make decisions for themselves. Mediation appreciates personal growth and promotes the notion that people can improve themselves and the world around them. It assumes that taking personal responsibility is a key to maturity and honorable behavior. Mediation philosophy acknowledges that people are continually learning and can be further enlightened by working through their problems with other people. Mediation is founded on a humanistic view of the world that does not accept that selfish and self-indulgent behaviors are inevitable features of the human condition.

These aspects of mediation make it appear to be akin to spirituality, gained through a therapeutic process. Although mediation does embrace the notion that the healing of conflict can lead to spiritual awakening, and the examination of self is quite therapeutic, mediation reflects another perspective as well. Mediation is also grounded in reality. It is centered around concrete problem solving. It attempts to identify a mutually acceptable truth for people in conflict. Mediation is about resolving disputes using the most practical and effective means available. Mediation attempts to avoid the convoluted labyrinth of the bureaucracy that forces people to engage in superfluous processes. Mediation is simple, to the point, practical, and efficient.

Perhaps these sound like contradictions, a process that is grounded in practical reality yet embraces human complexities. But this is not a contradiction; it is a true reflection of the human condition. People are complex mazes of ideas, feelings, and needs who nonetheless seek to be grounded in concrete reality. Many other means of dealing with problems ignore one reality or another. Either the process is removed from the emotional depth of the private person or it ignores the day-to-day need to be functional. Mediation attempts to address the complex in order to make it simple. It transposes the emotional into the rational, the chaotic into the orderly.

Understanding this philosophy is important because it is the guiding theory behind the practice. It helps to explain why a process that seems so simple and familiar is so unique. It articulates what many call the "magic" of mediation, the profound impact that this process has on a troubled situation, and why such a surprising result so often occurs. Mediation does not appear to be dramatically dissimilar from many other ways of handling problems, yet the satisfaction that follows is real, and genuinely different. Through mediation people resolve conflict, learn to be adept at preventing and addressing future problems, and gain a greater sense of satisfaction.

Still, mediation is not magic—it is merely a sound way to address problems. Mediation regards the complex nature of people. To understand mediation, it is important to learn both the ideology and the practical skills. Belief in the underlying theory does little good if there are no tools to make the process work.

Understanding mediation from a theoretical perspective is much different from working with live people with real problems. In mediation, as with many pursuits that involve helping people, the concepts and theories are only valuable when combined with useful skills, and these skills are more difficult to teach and learn than the concepts and theories behind them. The following sections address both the theoretical and the practical, but, most important, aim to ground the mediator with concrete techniques and interventions. In these sections new mediators can learn about the process and how to employ it.

The Mediator Role

A mediator is an impartial outsider who assists people in conflict to reach a consensus. A mediator has one primary goal: to assist the parties in dealing with their problem. Mediators serve in different capacities depending on the type of conflict, the attitudes of the parties, and the circumstances that arise during the mediation.

Mediations will vary, from formal settlement negotiations aimed at drafting a contract, to emotional therapeutic sessions with the goal of mending personal relationships. One factor that distinguishes mediation from other conflict resolution is the acknowledgment that a successful process can, and should, serve more than one purpose.

Although some mediation sessions focus on drafting contracts, and some require addressing only emotional concerns, many disputes demand divided attention. Mediation involves a holistic approach; it responds to both the business and personal side of conflict, so mediators must be prepared to address all circumstances that arise.

Workplace disputes are an excellent example of conflicts that often consist of business and personal issues. Due to attitudes and beliefs about appropriate workplace behavior, the parties may not always acknowledge this duality. One role of the mediator is to create an environment in which the parties are free to fully explore the problem and address concerns that might not otherwise be considered.

Creating an open and trusting environment is the mediator's responsibility. The parties may come to mediation with some distrust and hostility. They may feel apprehensive. This can easily translate into a stressful encounter, not conducive to agreement and understanding. The mediator must break through emotional barriers and set the stage for productive communication. To do this, a mediator demonstrates empathy, warmth, and faith in the people and the process.

Mediators have different personal styles and personality characteristics, and there is more than one appropriate way to design a comforting atmosphere. The mediator comes to mediation with specific techniques and ideas about how disputes can be resolved, but ultimately the mediator must be respectful and understanding of the parties' needs and desires and the individual path they wish to take.

STYLISTIC APPROACHES TO MEDIATION

Some mediators will take a more directive approach and some will be nondirective. There are numerous schools of thought on strategy. Mediators come from diverse backgrounds and have differing fundamental beliefs about problem solving. There is no universal prototype for addressing problems, but some methods are more appropriate for common situations.

Directive Approach

Mediation is generally not a forum in which outsiders make decisions for the disputing parties. Still, there are times when more directive approaches can be used in mediation. Perhaps the most important technique that can be adapted from legal practice is that of asking direct and clear questions. People in the legal field are experts at eliciting information through asking questions. Through direct and cross-examination thoughts are revealed that people may be unaware of, or are hiding.

Legal questioning tends to be directed from both an information gathering and confrontational approach. There may be a place in mediation for respectful confrontation, but traditional legal cross-examination is never an appropriate method for mediators. Cross-examination is designed to trick or trip a person into expressing what the examiner wants to hear. This may be a useful way to elicit factual information, but it tends to be humiliating and demonstrates a lack of trust or respect.

Mediators do want to encourage participants to challenge their preconceptions and perspectives, but they do not want to alienate or offend. It is not the mediators' prerogative to decide what must or even should be discussed. The mediator can suggest issues for discussion and may encourage the participants to communicate, but, ultimately, the parties have all the authority and autonomy to decide what will and will not be addressed.

What mediators can take from the legal perspective is the notion that specific questions and answers are only part of a whole that designs the truth, and that truth is different from different perspectives. Facts are only part of the truth, and even facts can be interpreted in many ways. When gathering information, the mediator is aware that answers to questions are merely pieces of a larger puzzle. The mediator can work with the parties to acknowledge that their own feelings and perceptions are only part of the truth and the truth will likely be different for other people. In recognizing this, a mediator can assist the parties to gain a more whole and objective perspective on their problem.

Nondirective Approach

The mediator's primary role is to create a safe environment in which the parties can express themselves freely—or not express themselves at all if that is their wish. A nondirective approach will often lead to the same outcome, a more whole and objective perspective. It is simply a different path. Some mediators believe that for the parties to maintain self-determination, or the right to make self-directed decisions, the mediator must not interfere with the course the parties take in mediation. Certain mediation modes restrict any mediator input that might alter the flow of discussion.

The nondirective approach is founded on the premise that the parties must learn to communicate more effectively with each other. Their inability to interact productively is harming the relationship and they must work through that block as a team. The mediator is less a problem solver and more a facilitator, creating an environment conducive to open communication. In this approach mediators may avoid caucusing, or private meetings, since the parties should be learning to work together. Mediators of this school believe that real growth can only occur when the people in conflict are communicating one-on-one. Since the purpose of this sort of mediation is to strengthen face-to-face communication, problems within mediation are handled face-to-face.

In a nondirective approach the role of the mediator is not always as clear as in a directive approach. Nondirective mediators allow the parties to dictate the flow of mediation. The parties set the ground rules themselves and the mediator tolerates emotional extremes. This method permits the parties to work though complex problems in an environment that is comfortable for them. The mediator does not impose. This makes a good deal of sense when the parties are motivated, highly verbal, and actively participate without prompting. Mediations of this type will more likely turn toward interpersonal and emotional issues, rather than contract negotiation. If the parties are willing and capable of engaging in this more personal work, and can do so in a productive fashion with self-awareness, nondirective mediation can lead to real personal growth and empowerment.

CHOOSING AN APPROACH

Nondirective mediation does not permit the mediator to use some tools that might benefit the parties by helping them to recognize hidden issues, or behaviors that continue to be unproductive. While it is imperative that mediation is conducted to suit the parties, the choices they have made previously have not resolved the dispute. In some instances, when lack of resolution has been caused by avoidance, offering an environment that permits discussion may be all that is needed. In many cases though, there are barriers to communication and resolution. Whether these barriers are emotional or related to more tangible requirements, the parties have not been able to devise a resolution method that works for them. Here, a more directive approach may be more effective.

Choosing to act as a directive or nondirective mediator depends in part on philosophical beliefs about the goals of mediation and the methods that effectively and ethically meet those goals. These philosophical beliefs or ideals are the seeds for models of practice, clearly defined styles that instruct the practitioner in appropriate strategies.

Related Disciplines

Mediators are instructed by other disciplines that deal with interpersonal intervention and have already designed sophisticated, complex, and varied models. Examples of practice models can be found in numerous fields. Social work, counseling, and psychology share models that are informative for the mediator.

Another example is the American legal system, which employs the adversarial model. The adversarial model is defined by an enormously complex set of principles and rules that offer the participants guidance and structure when working within the system. The adversarial system is based on an underlying philosophy that focuses on justice. Participants within the system all work within the same boundaries, accepting the same overriding philosophy: that the goal of solving problems is to achieve justice.

In counseling and psychotherapy, practitioners work from various therapeutic healing models. Therapeutic models are quite diverse and new approaches have emerged over time. These models are designed and applied using an underlying philosophy that meshes with the therapists' fundamental beliefs about human behavior. An example of a commonly known therapeutic method is the psychoanalytic model, based on biosocial and experiential theories of human behavior. The psychoanalytic model not only explains a philosophy of human behavior, but also instructs the therapist in appropriate techniques for intervening that honor the beliefs of the philosophy. Another recognizable therapeutic model is the cognitive-behavior approach. Based on dissimilar underlying assumptions than the psychoanalytic model, cognitive-behavioral techniques are very different, but also offer the practitioner a groundwork for defining and applying interventions.

Principles of Mediation

Mediation in the domestic-interpersonal conflict resolution arena, as opposed to international political mediation, is relatively young. The field is growing and is only beginning to clearly define models based on widely accepted philosophical principles. Rather than employing already defined models of practice, mediators often design a set of strategies that work for them based on philosophically sound principles of the field.

Neither the legal adversarial model nor any specific therapeutic model apply wholly to mediation. Mediation is based on philosophies of behavior and problem solving that have unique elements. Mediators need to design strategies that apply specifically to mediation goals. The first step in designing a model is to adopt general philosophical principles about the practice and goals of mediation, then apply those principles to practice techniques.

The following are some mediation principles to reflect upon. Each individual mediator can add to or alter this list to adapt it to philosophical or pragmatic requirements.

1. Mediation is aimed at resolving conflict in a way that satisfies the needs of the individual parties. The parties have a right to self-determination and to view the problem in a way that makes sense to them.

2. The mediator is a catalyst or facilitator in the mediation process and is not a judge, advocate, or authority.

3. The resolution of conflict encompasses more that a final agreement. The process of examining issues, strengthening relationships, and gaining greater understanding, insight, and empathy is an integral part of successful mediation.

4. The goal of mediation is broader than resolving the problem at hand. Mediation is a learning process and what is gained through mediation can be applied to relationships and conflicts in the future.

5. Mediation is a nonadversarial process, yet it respects that people will have divergent and competing perspectives and interests. Mediation is peaceful, nonviolent problem solving that addresses the different needs, wants, and desires of the participants.

6. Mediation accepts the notion that there is an emotional element to all conflict, that people are emotionally connected to all aspects of their lives, their work, and their beliefs. Exploring how personal feelings impact problems is therapeutic and valuable for reaching concrete agreements as well as for emotional healing.

7. Mediation aims to be time-efficient, cost-effective, and personally gratifying. While the mediation process can be difficult, the culmination of mediation should be satisfaction.

Adopting a Mediation Model

Adopting a mediation philosophy is instructive for making intervention decisions. Specific techniques are employed or avoided when working from a particular philosophy. A mediator develops strategies that are effective and reflect a particular perspective. When working within a framework, the mediator can preconceive techniques that fall within the appropriate parameters. This guides on-the-spot decision making.

Adopting an underlying philosophy or framework also cues the mediator to the boundaries of the intervention style. It helps the mediator to avoid instinctual, yet regrettable, responses. Mediation decisions are often made quickly without deliberation. An underlying philosophy offers a reference point. In a framework adopting a nondirective approach, a mediator will avoid offering advice. If, for instance, a situation should occur in which advice is requested, the mediator can reflect on the adopted philosophy—in this case one that supports self-determination—and be guided in making a response.

A mediation philosophy also underlies the behavior that is modeled by the mediator. Modeling functional behavior is a tool widely used by mediators. When the parties observe appropriate and productive communication, they are prompted to act in a similar manner. It is assumed that people learn from observation and benefit from watching healthy interaction. A mediator should consider a framework that offers the best opportunity for modeling functional behavior.

Directive and nondirective approaches model different styles of behavior. If a mediator is nondirective, hesitant to offer constructive insight, there is less affirmative behavior being modeled that the parties can emulate. Nondirective mediators model respect, concern, and empathy, all very positive practices. Some parties will benefit greatly from witnessing a yielding and respectful attitude, particularly if the parties have a history of incessant bickering.

Other useful techniques that the mediator can model require a more directive approach. Respectful challenging, forthright questioning, and open expression of emotion, feelings, thoughts, and ideas all come with a more directive style. The choice of which philosophy to adopt generally reflects the beliefs of the mediator and the needs of the parties.

JOBS OF THE MEDIATOR

Whatever style of mediation is employed, the mediator always permits the parties to speak as needed, in an open and inviting atmosphere. Quite often what has been most lacking for the disputants is a forum to be heard. For these participants mediation becomes that forum, and the mediator encourages the parties to speak freely and openly about whatever is on their minds. A mediator tempers the open environment to some degree, which varies depending on the mediation philosophy. Certainly the parties never have complete freedom to attack each other.

Setting Ground Rules

One way a mediator creates a safe environment is by acting as a buffer between people who are harboring hostilities. Some mediators set clear ground rules at the start of mediation and request that the parties allow each other to talk without interruption and refrain from aggressive or disrespectful speech. Other mediators do not believe it is the mediator's job to impose such a structure, since the parties should be free to speak openly about anything that concerns them. The amount of structure imposed on the process depends on the philosophy and personal style of the mediator. It will vary somewhat from case to case, depending on the behavior of the participants.

In setting ground rules, the mediator acknowledges that parties are currently entrenched in a problem that they have not been able to effectively address. The parties are looking to the mediator for freedom to express themselves, coupled with protection from attack. The parties see the mediator as an experienced and knowledgeable authority figure, not a judge or critic. The mediator has the capacity to rein in a problem so it can be dealt with rationally and productively.

Other Duties

The mediator has additional duties, some very practical. In the most basic sense, the mediator runs the mediation. The mediator organizes chairs and tables, sets the mood, describes procedures, and assures nervous people. The mediator directs the mediation, may set ground rules, and orchestrates the flow of conversation. The mediator helps to draw out information and hidden or confused feelings by asking questions. The mediator also recognizes posturing and assists to initiate honest communication. In some instances the mediator helps to quiet squabbles by redirecting communication when people are disruptive or combative. Despite the fact that the mediator has no decision-making authority, the mediator has the power of influence.

All mediators must learn how to perform these functions, while honoring a mediation philosophy and adapting to the needs of the individual parties. As with any interpersonal activity, mediations will differ; there is no script. Even so, mediators develop a philosophy, a personal style, and body of knowledge that helps to predict what will occur during mediation. This knowledge helps the mediator guide the parties toward a productive session.

GAINING PROFICIENCY

The following are concepts that help to describe the proficient mediator. These concepts are instructive for the mediator who is examining personal beliefs and skills.

A proficient mediator enjoys problem solving in emotionally stressful situations. Mediating a conflict requires becoming intimately involved with the parties' problems, which always involve emotional elements. Even disputes regarding business agreements or contracts are colored by issues of personal competence, self-worth, fairness, and morality. In addition, business disputes always reflect some amount of personal and professional risk. Other types of disputes are even more emotionally charged.

A mediator must remain focused, patient, empathetic, and rational in the heat of any emotional encounter. Simultaneously, a mediator also must recognize and sometimes highlight the emotional components of a problem when they exist, even when the parties are not aware of them. The mediator helps to sift through the emotional mire, and assists the parties in making distinctions about what issues are necessary and productive to explore. Emotional and interpersonal confusion is often stressful for the parties and in turn stressful for the mediator.

A proficient mediator enjoys problem solving in intellectually stressful situations. In addition to the complexity of the emotional and interpersonal issues that emerge during mediation, challenging questions may arise about the substantive subject matter of the problem. Mediations in the workplace can potentially involve workplace policy, legal or administrative issues, technical subject matter related to the work performed, health or medical questions, harassment or discrimination concerns, and other issues.

In most mediations, the mediator does not need to be an expert or even knowledgeable about the mediation subject matter. The mediator does need to be able and willing to learn. In most instances the parties have all the information and knowledge necessary to solve the problem, even if they don't presently agree on a solution. The parties can teach the mediator everything that is necessary to deal with the issues, provided the mediator is able to ask appropriate questions, recognize confusion, and check for flaws in the analysis. The mediator must accept the challenge of learning new and sometimes complex information. This often requires sifting through information with the parties to determine what is truly relevant and what is missing.

A proficient mediator realizes that people have good reasons for their behavior. Despite what an outsider or hindsight might reveal, from the perspective of the people entrenched in an ongoing conflict, their previous responses to the predicament have made sense. They are attempting to address the dilemma in a way that seems rational within their repertoires of coping behaviors.

All people have had problems that seem difficult or even impossible to solve. In dealing with these difficult problems, people employ strategies that are within their knowledge and experience. Some of these strategies prove to be effective and some are not. Personal agendas vary from problem to problem, but, regardless of the outcome, the intention is always to satisfy a need, to address the problem in a way that makes sense.

It is true that some problem-solving strategies are more effective than others; some are more rational, some are less likely to cause residual harm, and some may be more honorable or ethical. But all attempts to solve a problem are genuine and aimed at serving some perceived legitimate purpose. A mediator must regard all attempts as the best attempts that the people are capable of or willing to make at that time.

It is useful for the mediator to assume that the people involved in the conflict are doing the best they can. A critical or judgmental attitude will more likely evoke self-defense than initiate an open dialogue. On a personal level, the mediator does not have to admire the behavior that is displayed; a mediator may find it offensive, unjust, childish, and wholly unproductive, but that does not negate the fact that the situation, as it stands, is reality for those people. To contradict motivation or behavior in a way that questions integrity or rational thought will be destructive to the mediator and participant relationship. The mediator is not a moral authority or judge of character, but rather an aide who steps into the world of the participants solely for the purpose of assisting them to fix a problem, in a way satisfactory to them.

A proficient mediator realizes that the parties have often given a great deal of thought to their problem. Calling on an outsider to assist in resolving a problem is a dramatic move that is not entered into lightly. By the time a mediator becomes involved, the problem has proven to be unresolvable and has become significant enough to warrant intervention by an outsider. But the fact that the problem is beyond the parties' capabilities to resolve does not mean they haven't been working diligently on their own. Although some people deal with problems by disregarding them, most people spend a great deal of time ruminating over conflicts. In fact, for many people problems that seem unresolvable take on an exaggerated importance. People often obsess over conflict and consider the issues thoroughly, at least as thoroughly as their limited personal perspective will allow. This may be the key to why many conflicts are difficult to resolve independently.

When people spend an inordinate amount of time considering a problem, but only have a limited amount of information, lacking the perspective of the other side, the conflict can become distorted. The parties may need assistance in gaining clarity. They need an opportunity to gain insight into other perspectives. They must step back and reexamine the issues in a new light. However, none of this reflects a lack of forethought.

The mediator does have the benefit of objectivity and the insight that can result. However, the mediator is not an expert on the problem, the circumstances that parties must contend with, the relationship between the people, or the consequences of any particular resolution. The mediator must allow the parties to instruct, evincing neither condescension nor impatience. The mediator learns from the expertise of the parties and in turn helps them to gain clarity and further awareness.

A proficient mediator realizes and accepts that the people presenting the conflict have the greatest understanding of the problem. When viewing a problem with distance, it is often much easier to be objective and rational. It is also easier to make judgments about what is just, fair, and reasonable. This outlook can be both a help and a hindrance for a mediator. While it is helpful for the parties to gain the perspective of an objective outsider, an outsider may lack insight into the emotions or other underlying issues that influence the behavior and thinking of the people in conflict. There is really no way an outsider, with limited knowledge of the people and all the elements that make up the dilemma, can fully appreciate the complexities of the problem.

Most interpersonal problems consist of more than the surface disagreement. The emotional foundation of the conflict brings into play the personalities of the people involved, their past experiences, personal beliefs, and individual requirements, which may or may not be openly expressed. Less overtly emotional conflicts, such as business disputes, involve the same human dimensions. One dispute might hinge on the way a person believes he or she should be treated and reflects past experience with power relationships. Another dispute might hinge on the desire to make larger amounts of money in order to support a family or foster a sense of personal accomplishment and power. These issues reflect personal beliefs about success and the work ethic.

An effective mediator remembers that an outsider cannot impose his or her judgment on those whose problem it is. The mediator's role is to assist the parties in bringing the relevant issues to light, then aid in making judgments about what is important and where the focus should lie. The mediator may offer insight, but only as a reflection of what the parties are expressing, not as an imposition of ideas that come solely from the mediator's personal perspective. The mediator may engage the parties in strategies for problem solving developed in previous disputes, but these strategies must be applied in a way that is relevant and respectful of the parties' stated needs.

A proficient mediator is curious about patterns of behavior and what motivates actions. Behavior is a complex. From the perspective of an outsider, certain behavior may appear rash or irrational. But from the perspective of the person behaving, it makes sense. Generally speaking, behavior reflects the best response available to that person. There is some underlying motivator that leads a person to act in a certain way. Most people have a tendency to repeat behaviors, to respond to similar situations in similar ways, even if these responses have not proven to be productive in the past. Learning to recognize behavior patterns, and then to alter patterns when they are ineffective, is very difficult.

Mediation is, in part, an examination of what people do and why they do it. Through self-examination individuals are able to make alternative choices when unable to attain desired results. While mediation is certainly not psychoanalysis, it is concerned with interpretations of the self and others. Mediation does not examine behavior to the depth of many therapy models, but practitioners are still interested in identifying why people do things, what the outcomes of actions will be, and how people adapt actions to better obtain desirable results.

A mediator is concerned with this search and finds it compelling. Mediators are curious about what motivates people and what promotes action or inaction. The participants will come to mediation with different levels of self-awareness. Some people will be keenly aware of what motivates and blocks them. For these people the mediator can work to help find comfortable alternatives. Other people will have little personal insight. For these people the mediator can gently probe into what might affect their actions and feelings. The mediator is not expected to alter personalities or perspectives on the world. But the mediator can help people more clearly understand why they do things, how their choices affect them and other people, and what are the most productive and satisfying ways to behave.

A proficient mediator understands that all behavior has a history and that history is a story. Patterns of behavior are not random. Behavior is a product of personal history. A mediator understands that there is a rational progression that precedes action. A person can delve deeply into background and examine childhood, or can explore more recent history and interpret problems by assessing present relationships. The depth to which history is explored depends on the circumstances. In most instances examination reflects the history that clearly encapsulates the conflict, such as the interpersonal and professional dynamics between the parties, the circumstances of the dispute, and the steps that have already been taken to address the problem.

The mediator appreciates that all interaction has a history, long or short. History is told as a story. It is a personal and collective interpretation of events that can be shaped. In hearing other people's interpretations of common events, it is evident that not everyone's interpretation of history is the same. In fact, stories that describe events always differ depending on the teller. The truth lies in the memory and interpretation. Throughout life, the interpretation of history changes with altered memory and perspective. History is a collection of stories; these stories change over time.

A proficient mediator understands that problems are related as stories. Since stories are expressed differently over time, the way problems are interpreted changes. In an attempt to address a dilemma, it is reinterpreted many times. Different theories will be applied to a problem in assessing who is responsible and how it can be resolved. Analyzing conflict is not a simple task because interpretations change. Upon reflection there will be shifts in conception. A single predicament may produce conflicting emotions. For instance, anger, frustration, sadness, pity, and indifference may all be experienced in working through a problem. An obstacle may at one time feel overwhelming and later become insignificant. Changes in the conception of a situation can reflect the fluctuating behavior of other people or a newly conceived perspective. Problems, which are both concrete and conceptual, are never stagnant.

Problems are a manifestation of internal and external stories. Because of the mutable nature of stories, and since problems are the manifestation of stories, problems change, either by chance or by design. When stories are reinterpreted, the problem is altered. The mediator and the participants work together to reform the stories that describe the conflict. This is done through reframing ideas, gathering new information, gaining empathy, exploring alternative options, and clarifying requirements. Through this process the parties redefine the conflict and create a situation that is more satisfying. By changing the stories that define the conflict, perspective on resolution can change.

A proficient mediator, through questions, helps to shift the pattern of the disagreement. When the pattern of debate is broken, the parties are free to reinterpret the issues and form new perspectives. During a disagreement there is a tendency for people to take strong positions and remain steadfast about those positions regardless of whether or not it best serves their goals. There are several factors that promote this position taking: an interest in serving a perceived justice; the desire to save face or pride; an inability to see other perspectives as a result of anger, fear, or pain; or simply a drive to win. Although these are not irrational motivations, they do not necessarily lead to the most effective or efficient resolutions. There are certainly times when remaining adamant about a position is the virtuous path, but, other times, if the pattern of thinking on an issue can be altered, there will be great gains.

When one is stuck in a pattern of thinking, it is very difficult to independently reconceptualize. When shifted patterns of thinking do occur, it is often out of a fear of losing or an acceptance of defeat. This is not a true reconceptualization, but rather a concession, which brings with it a host of new problems, such as resentment or humiliation and a loss of personal power.

When the pattern of thinking underlying the disagreement is shifted before there is a winner and loser, then it is possible to reinterpret the situation in a way that satisfies mutual needs. For this reinterpretation to occur the parties must be willing and able to reassess their goals or redefine their stories about the problem. The mediator can assist the parties to move beyond the rut of the debate and adamant positions.

A mediator brings to the interaction an objective and nonjudgmental perspective that is not motivated by personal gain. The mediator can open new lines of dialogue without appearing self-aggrandizing, as might an opponent. And the mediator can do so without coercing, belittling, or threatening power positions. The mediator, as an objective outsider, can assist the parties to move away from stalemate without losing.

A competent mediator understands that if the parties could resolve the dispute on their own, they would not have sought help. While a mediator does not want to threaten self-determination, the parties have sought the assistance of the mediator because they have been unable to reach the goals they desire. The mediator is an important part of a team. The fact that the mediator remains neutral or impartial does not require the mediator to be inactive. The parties expect the mediator to be an expert in resolving conflict. The mediator has come to this process with special skills and a unique perspective that the parties do not possess.

Although the mediator never judges or mandates action, the mediator is still perceived as an authority figure. The mediator is an authority in resolving conflict and the parties count on this to be true. The parties, who have been involved in a difficult, if not overwhelming dilemma, are relieved to have the aid of an expert assistant. When coming to mediation, the parties need and want help. The mediator should not be afraid to demonstrate confidence; the parties expect and appreciate it.

While beginning mediators may not feel the level of confidence and competence of more experienced practitioners, the benefit of objectivity and an unencumbered perspective are great assets. A fresh viewpoint alone will comfort and aid the parties. And even beginning mediators have been exposed to theory and practice skills that are otherwise unavailable to the parties. All mediators have much to offer the parties and mediators should embrace their authority, not in order to control, but rather to offer guidance and act as a team leader when parties are in need of direction.

In addition to the considerations above, a proficient mediator is constantly learning and considering the process anew. Mediators embrace the philosophy of mediation and learn through experience how beneficial the process can be. A belief in the process and a genuine regard for the parties is dramatically important for the effective mediator. This care and consideration will have a great impact. The more thoughtful the mediator is about the process, the more this dedication will come across. A conscientious and dedicated mediator will have no trouble building a strong rapport and trust, which inevitably leads to success in communication and resolution.

Impartiality

Impartiality, or what is frequently called neutrality, reflects the same concept—the idea that the mediator does not take sides. Maintaining impartiality or neutrality is essential for successful mediation. Remaining unbiased is a principle function of the mediator. The presence of an unbiased third party mediator defines the mediation process. It is precisely because of the impartiality or neutrality of the mediator that mediation is a unique process.

Preserving an unbiased viewpoint is a significant concern for all mediators. It is a concept that mediation instructors impress on new mediators and all working mediators highlight to the parties. Yet, despite the importance of this function, or perhaps because of its importance, the concepts of impartiality and neutrality punctuate some complex issues.

IMPARTIALITY VERSUS NEUTRALITY

Analyzed carefully, neutrality and impartiality are not synonymous. True neutrality demands refraining from any intervention that might challenge the perceptions of the parties. Impartiality suggests only that the mediator does not support one position over another, or impose his or her own positions. Impartiality allows the mediator to challenge perceptions and offer an array of alternative interpretations.

For this reason, "impartiality" is preferred by those who acknowledge that the mediator engages in proactive challenges that encourage the parties to reevaluate their predetermined notions of the problem. Notwithstanding terminology, the problem remains the same. A mediator must face the challenge of respecting the mandate, to allow people to make their own decisions, while at the same time proactively helping them challenge their perceptions and interpretations.

MAINTAINING IMPARTIALITY

It is the mediator's responsibility to act impartially at all times. The mediator must not foster the impression that he or she is taking sides on any issue. The complete confidence of the parties in the mediator's lack of bias toward either side is essential for a successful mediation.

While this is true, it is not easy for a mediator to maintain strict impartiality at all times. In developing sound mediator skills it is important to consider what exactly impartiality is, what techniques can be employed to maintain it, and what might be a threat to this standard.

Although impartiality is usually described as an affirmative action—"the mediator must be impartial" or "the mediator should act in a neutral manner"—it is very difficult to describe the actions of a nonaction. The phrase "act neutral" does not offer much practical guidance. How does one act out something they are not supposed to do? Rather than quantifying or illustrating impartiality, it is easier to describe issues that affect the ability to maintain impartiality.

Personal Responses to Conflict

Consider what human and individual personal characteristics might stand in the way of impartial behavior. No one comes to mediation with a completely clear mind. No matter how objective a person attempts to be, it is impossible to escape the fact that by nature people make judgments. Views that are ingrained into personal conception are difficult to disregard. Further, people who are inclined to become mediators are likely to have strong intellectual and emotional responses to the types of issues that arise during mediation. These responses may stem from well-considered opinions or gut feelings. Mediators are smart and sensitive about conflict and concerned with many of the issues that reoccur in mediations.

Self-Examination. Mediators tend to have strong ideas about issues that commonly lead to mediation. To become involved as a mediator there must be an interest in human behavior and conflict. This interest frequently leads to a sensitivity about others as well as an inclination toward self-examination. Propensity toward self-examination is useful for identifying those impulses that must be controlled. Mediators must refrain from imposing personal perceptions. Although mediators may have strongly held beliefs, they are well equipped to identify inappropriate interjections.

Biases. Biases are natural and unavoidable. Acknowledging predilections makes it easier to recognize when they might cloud judgment. Harboring a bias does not presuppose that the bias must invade the process. A mediator can, and must, control inclinations toward using personal bias, beliefs, or prejudices to affect negotiations. Issues that involve personal morality tend to pose the most risk. Mediation is not an appropriate forum for moral or ethical teaching, unless enlightenment comes through exploration initiated by the parties. If a mediator feels that objectivity will be compromised due to a strongly held belief or a bias, the mediator must excuse him or herself from the process.

Successful Impartiality

The key to successful impartiality is maintaining the distinction between making observations and making judgments. Inquiring about the thoughts, feelings, and intentions of a person is not akin to judging them. Mediators are interpreters. Mediators listen and explore. Mediators summarize, rephrase, and interpret. Mediators may make suggestions, but never belittle, intimidate, or coerce.

In addition to acting unbiased, a mediator must appear nonjudgmental. In taking affirmative steps to elicit information and feelings, a mediator must be wary of misinterpretation. Defensiveness, emotional fragility, or simple confusion may lead a participant to misread the intention of the mediator. Inquiry may be interpreted as judgment. Misunderstanding is a common cause of conflict.

Asking Questions. The phrasing of questions will have an impact on the participants. Questions should be posed in a neutral manner; they should not imply a judgment. Prefacing a question with a nonthreatening remark can diminish the risk that a question will be interpreted as a confrontation. By starting questions with phrases such as: "I am curious," "I am confused," "I may misunderstand you," or "Can you help me understand?," a mediator can challenge an idea without appearing to challenge the integrity of the speaker. To remove any aggressive implications, adopt a curious or concerned attitude. Never say, "You need to"; instead say, "Would you consider." Don't say, "That is not what you said before"; say, "I am wondering about what you just said."

Addressing Lying. People are not always completely truthful when presenting their stories. Sometimes people lie. Other times people will allow themselves to believe things that are false. Presenting a story that is untrue may be an attempt to manipulate. Manipulation is a self-protective barrier, a dysfunctional struggle to address a difficult situation. The manipulator fears the response that a straightforward approach will elicit. This person believes that forthright communication will result in a negative consequence. This belief is most likely based on some previous experience. Although manipulation is offensive, in the mind of the manipulator there is a legitimate reason for this strategy.

It is not productive to confront a lying or manipulative person. It is not the role of the mediator to dismantle self-protective barriers. A mediator should instead use empathy and tact to support an interaction where these defenses are not needed. It is the mediator's job to assist in finding a less caustic strategy, but the mediator should do this without accusations. Again, prefacing an inquiry with a nonthreatening remark can diminish the risk that it will be interpreted as a confrontation.

Mediation and Advocacy

Mediators make a clear distinction between mediation and advocacy. All practitioners accept the premise that a mediator must be impartial, must not give legal advice, and must not act as an advocate. Even practitioners who work as advocates in other arenas, such as law or human services, follow these restrictions when in the role of mediator. Some states have implemented statutory ethical guidelines requiring mediators to adhere to these standards. Professional mediator organizations also insist that mediators refrain from engaging in practices that violate these principles.

ENCOURAGEMENT

Encouragement is often used by the mediator as a tool to promote negotiation. Mediators encourage parties to appreciate the perspectives of the other side in an attempt to motivate settlements. Sometimes this encouragement is subtle and may not be intentional; other times it is overt. It is clear that mediators are not permitted to explicitly advocate for one side. Encouragement and advocacy are not synonymous. Encouragement, while it may be perceived as advocacy, is integral to some styles of mediation and is effective and welcome.

When encouraging, a mediator does not advocate the soundness of any position, but rather supports the examination and appreciation of all interpretations. A mediator should feel free to encourage the parties, make them feel their ideas are valuable, their feelings are appreciated, and their positions are sound. A mediator may also encourage one side to reflect on the stance of another.

IMPROPER ADVOCACY

A debate within the field continues over whether certain strategies should be universally banned from mediation practice. Mediators are prohibited from providing legal or other technical advice, but mediators do sometimes offer their insight. Very often the parties desire this sort of assistance and directly request it. Lawyers and nonlawyers alike are frequently asked to contribute personal or professional opinions during mediation, presenting a dilemma for a mediator who wishes to be helpful. Mediators should take into consideration whether their input will sway the outcome of mediation. In making an assessment, the mediator must not advocate for a position.

Arbitrators

There are some practices that are mislabeled mediation and clearly violate its fundamental principles. Perhaps the most blatant breach of mediation principles is executing arbitration in the name of mediation. Arbitration is essentially a mini-trial. The arbitrator hears evidence and renders a binding decision. With the agreement of the parties, the arbitrator acts as a judge. Although it is unlikely that an arbitrator would intentionally mislead the parties into believing that arbitration is mediation, sometimes mediators behave like arbitrators. This is most likely to occur when lawyers act as mediators and have difficulty escaping their adversarial inclinations. These lawyers may unintentionally cross-examine or present a legal judgment, performing in the role of advocate or arbiter.

Helping Practitioners

Practitioners from other disciplines are also at risk for slipping into the role of advocate. In many therapeutic models the counselor promotes certain behavior and compels clients to perform tasks or exercises. Helping practitioners who work with children or the disabled sometimes design behavior plans that mandate action. They also advocate on behalf of their clients in the community. These practitioners may find it challenging to escape the role of advocate when working with mediation participants.

Workplace Peer Mediators

In the workplace, peer mediators may have knowledge or experience that will lead them to have strong opinions about the efficacy of resolutions. Workplace peer mediators may be familiar with workplace policy, typical workplace attitudes and behavior, the workplace culture, and the people involved in the dispute. This insight may contribute to preconceptions or misgivings about decisions made during mediation. Workplace peer mediators will likewise need to avoid advocating for positions that support personal assessments.

Regardless of professional background or experience, it is difficult to avoid embracing a position or a solution that seems clearly functional or just. Mediators will be swayed by the arguments of some participants and will be inclined to align with that side. There will also be occasions in which the mediator dislikes a participant or disdains their attitude. It is natural to support or reject particular points of view. However, a mediator must be careful not to allow past experience or present perceptions to unduly influence negotiations.

Mediation and Therapy

Mediation is described as a therapeutic process, but is distinguished from therapy. Mediation models are different from traditional therapy models and mediators do not consider themselves therapists. Because mediation deals with personal and interpersonal concerns, emotions underlie many disputes and are frequently addressed during mediation. While a mediator is not a therapist, mediators do draw from theories of human behavior and counseling techniques. A mediator should not confuse a mediation session with psychological counseling, but mediators can learn a great deal from therapists about how to assist troubled people while remaining objective, rational, sincere, honest, and sane.

Mediators sometimes adamantly oppose the notion that mediation be compared to therapy or counseling. This strong stance may be shortsighted because it discounts the well-developed and successful body of therapeutic modalities that can inform mediation. Some mediators are not familiar with advances in psychotherapeutic practice and think of therapy from a very narrow and traditional perspective. Therapy is no longer limited to years of psychoanalysis or dozens of psychotherapy sessions where the patient uncovers childhood trauma. Brief therapy may last only a few sessions, taking a problem-solving approach and sharing the philosophical and pragmatic characteristics of mediation. Mediation does share some of the tools of these newer therapy techniques.

The following is a summary of some relevant therapeutic approaches. This list is not all-inclusive and is only an overview of theory and technique. Any person serious about developing counseling skills for mediation would benefit greatly from exploring these and other therapeutic models in greater depth.

INDIVIDUAL THERAPY THEORIES

Person-Centered Therapy

Person or client-centered therapy is an outgrowth of Carl Rogers' theories of human psychology and behavior. Rogers' thinking diverged from traditional conceptualizations of psychoanalytic or Freudian theory. Propounding a more humanistic approach, Rogers believed that people have great potential for growth and change, and that self-understanding comes from within. Rogers believed in the inherent trustworthiness of people. In the person-centered approach, the client is responsible for self-discovery and awareness. Person-centered therapy is not behavioral; it is not task oriented. The goal is not action but rather *actualization* or awareness.

Rogers did not believe that the therapist should be directive and authoritarian, but rather should be nurturing and compassionate. He believed in the possibility of dynamic personal change, facilitated by a partnership between a therapist and client, sharing a genuine and honest interaction. It is the therapists' job to travel on a mutual journey with a client, sometimes acting as a gentle guide, but always respecting the wishes and perceptions of the client. The therapist focuses less on technique and more on attitude. Authentic expression of nonjudgmental caring and empathy is used to break down defensive barriers. The primary tools of the therapist are active listening, unconditional acceptance, demonstrating respect, expressing empathetic understanding, and responding in a noncontrived, fluid, and genuine manner. As a result of person-centered therapy, a client will theoretically move toward more functional behaviors (Corey, 1996; Newfield, 2000).

Gestalt Therapy

Gestalt therapy, developed by Fritz Perls, is rooted in existential philosophy and phenomenology, or personal awareness and individual reality. In this model all people are considered personally responsible for their own destiny. Gestalt therapy concentrates on the *here and now*. Focus is placed on present thoughts and feelings. Participants are encouraged to feel rather than think; clients experience rather than analyze. The focus is on what is occurring, not why it is happening. The key to success in gestalt therapy is awareness.

A genuine and personal relationship between the therapist and client is extremely important in gestalt therapy. However, the client has a great deal of responsibility in the relationship and should not rely on the therapist for insight and answers. Gestalt therapists believe that people are responsible for their own problems and have the capacity to make personal change. It is our lack of connection to reality that binds us. Personal growth occurs when we face our own reality and deal with our problems in an honest, open, and straightforward manner.

Gestalt therapists are particularly concerned with unfinished business or unexpressed feelings and becoming stuck, thus avoiding our reality and seeking out others in destructive ways. Change comes with knowing and accepting oneself and others and making genuine connections. To reach this stage we must stop avoiding reality, work though our complex system of neuroses, make contact with ourselves and others, and focus on what is called our *energy*.

Gestalt techniques include assisting clients to become more self-aware by making observations, guiding, gentle confrontation, and initiating exercises. Gestalt exercises have been well developed and are an important part of therapy. Therapists often ask clients to speak through their bodies. Gestalt therapists are particularly aware of body language and look for unspoken messages. Gestalt therapists challenge clients in a considerate manner, they prompt *I statements*, or speaking in the first person. They also look for hidden messages in stories and will ask questions to draw out individual truth. In sum, gestalt therapy is a fluid and open dialogue between therapist and client, in a search for awareness through authentic contact (Becvar & Becvar, 1996; Corey, 1996).

Reality Therapy

Reality therapy, based on control theory and developed by William Glasser, also focuses on individual perceptions and the notion that we are personally responsible to shape our lives. This theory proposes that we define our world by our basic human needs in conjunction with our interpretation of reality. Glasser defines these basic needs as: *belonging, power, freedom, fun,* and *physiological survival.* Our behavior is an attempt to control the external world to satisfy our basic needs. Glasser believes that we attempt to make the external world conform with our internal perceptions of what the world should be. Because we define and control our own worlds, we have the power to change.

Reality therapy is designed to help people get what they really want out of life, or attain a *quality world.* Glasser believes that we actively create our lives. In fact, Glasser goes so far as to contend that metal illness is coping behavior and merely an attempt, albeit a misguided one, to satisfy needs. Because behavior is a choice, we can choose to live differently, although, changing is hard work and to change requires taking active responsibility.

In reality therapy the therapist takes a partnership role founded on trust. The therapist serves as a teacher, giving direction, making observations, and offering suggestions of alternative ways to behave. Reality therapists acknowledge that all behavior is an honest attempt to satisfy needs, but troubled individuals have made ineffective choices. Along with a safe and open therapeutic environment, reality therapists employ specific strategies. Therapists ask questions to identify what a client *wants.* Current behavior is isolated and examined in an exercise called *direction and doing.* Then clients *evaluate* the effectiveness of behavior. And, finally, clients plan strategies for changing behavior and agree to effectuate change, steps called *planning and commitment* (Corey, 1996; Newfield, 2000).

Cognitive-Behavior Therapy

Cognitive-behavior therapy is a heading that includes a number of approaches that all share common theoretical principles. Cognitive behavior in some form is the most widely used therapeutic model today; perhaps because it is quite inclusive and incorporates components from numerous schools of thought. It can be applied in either a rigid or flexible manner, with more or less direction from the therapist, depending on the circumstances. All cognitive-behavioral approaches focus on thought, learning, and action. In each form there is a collaborative relationship between therapist and client.

The basic premise is that dysfunction is related to cognitive or thought processing, and a change in thinking is necessary to effectuate a change in behavior. Specific educational and action-oriented techniques are used to target problem thinking and, in turn, change behavior.

Rational emotive behavior therapy (REBT), a term coined by Albert Ellis, is one cognitive-behavioral approach. In REBT it is assumed that people have capacities for rational and logical thinking and for irrational and confused thinking. Although people wish to have successful and happy relationships and positive self-concepts, there is an inherent propensity for self-destruction as well. Negative tendencies may be ingrained by viewing the world in absolutist terms, using *shoulds, musts,* and *oughts*. These irrational notions promote failure, or at least a sense of failure. In REBT, just as we can foster self-defeating thinking, we can nurture self-affirming thinking. Through rational thinking and acting we change our feelings about who we are.

The therapists' role is that of educator and director. Although REBT therapists do develop trusting, nonjudgmental relationships with clients, REBT is a directive approach. Therapists encourage changes in thinking patterns, point out irrational notions, use logic to persuade, and demonstrate the destructive consequences of irrational thinking. REBT therapists assign homework and exercises for practicing new cognitive patterns. In essence, REBT is an educational approach with the goal of restructuring thought processes; when we believe differently, we behave differently, and then feel differently (Becvar & Becvar, 1996; Corey, 1996).

FAMILY THERAPY THEORIES

Loosely defined, a workplace is analogous to a family. Many people spend two-thirds of their waking hours at their jobs and spend years interacting with the same coworkers. People form emotional attachments and have power struggles. They strive to make relationships functional in order to meet important goals, such as growth, stability, success, achievement, and satisfaction. Working people grapple with the balance of meeting personal needs while satisfying coworkers and an employer. All people who work must abide by the rules of the workplace society, and at the same time remain true to themselves.

Because the workplace dynamic is akin to the family dynamic, strategies to resolve problems in the home can also apply to work. There is a separate body of therapeutic models designed specifically for serving families. The following describes the basic structure of some important family therapy models.

Structural Family Therapy

Structural Family Therapy, identified by Salvador Minuchin, works under a model that is based on a *family systems theory*. Systemically oriented therapies explore the interconnectedness of people. In a systems approach, a person's position on a problem is affected by their relationships with other people. Positions are solidified with the support of an outside influence.

Families are seen as part of the larger society or interrelationship of systems. Families are not independent entities but rather take cues from the complex outside world. There is interaction between the family and outside systems, and each family member has independent relationships with outside systems. Since the world is not static, and families are constantly influenced by the world, families are always evolving and changing. Because of this proclivity toward change, therapists know that shifts in the behavior and thinking of family members will lead to change in the family structure.

Structural therapists accept the reality that there is a hierarchy of power in a family. Different members have, and should have, different levels of authority. The goal is to work toward functional relationships in which power is neither misplaced nor abused, where all family members are working toward maximum individual growth and mutual support of the family. It is understood that family members have expectations of each other, and when these expectations are not met, there is a tendency to blame and use guilt as a tool to manipulate. Structural therapists seek to find more productive tools to orchestrate change. For the structural therapist, manipulation is not a negative concept, it is the maneuvering of interactions and relationships, which, if done in a positive and productive fashion, leads to functional systems.

The specific tools of the structural therapist include many of the same tools used by mediators. Structuralists are concerned with identifying patterns. The family is encouraged to demonstrate patterns that the therapist observes. The therapist also takes a leadership role, giving direction, highlighting and restructuring patterns. The structural therapist is concerned with boundaries and personal space, with redirecting stress, and with joining or redefining alliances and coalitions. The structural therapist works with the family to assign tasks or, in essence, to write a contract. The therapist works to redefine or relabel the problem so it will be perceived differently. And, finally, the therapist supports or reinforces competence and success, helping build confidence, trust, and self-esteem (Becvar & Becvar, 1996; Kilpatrick & Holland, 1995; Newfield, 2000).

Strategic Therapy

Strategic therapy, conceived by Jay Haley and Cloé Madanes, is also used as a way to help families overcome problems. But, unlike structural therapy, it is not founded on systematic dysfunction. Strategic therapists view neuroses as problems in need of solutions. Strategic therapy is process-oriented, focused on finding solutions to problems rather than gaining insight or awareness. This is a directive approach and the therapist is seen as an expert in charge of the interactions that occur during sessions. The ultimate goal is to change behavior; any change in thinking or understanding is an aside that occurs as a result of the behavioral change.

This theory focuses a great deal on power relationships. There is an assumption that the family suffers from dysfunctional power relationships and therefore the therapist must take control. Strategic therapy does not focus on communication techniques. Rather, the therapist plans strategies that the family follows; much of the planning and strategy is done in a covert or secret manner. Using this technique, the therapist takes the primary responsibility for designing and initiating change. From the strategic therapist's perspective, if the clients were capable of change on their own, they would not need a therapist. Therapy is not about teaching people how to change, but rather about causing change to occur. Strategic therapy accomplishes change.

Strategic therapists are interested in symbolic behavior; they use theatrics, pretending, and rituals that highlight symbolic change. Family members are often assigned tasks to accomplish that effect change in behavior and also symbolize change. Completing tasks alters problem behavior; it also demonstrates to others that change is desired and real action is being undertaken. Strategic therapists rely heavily on *paradoxical interventions*. These are directives that require a client to exaggerate a problem behavior. A paradox is often used when a person is demonstrating resistance to help. Change occurs when the behavior is no longer rewarding or becomes absurd. Finally, strategic therapists reframe or reinterpret problems. Often, when a problem is given a new meaning, it is no longer seen as a problem and the issues are much easier to address (Becvar & Becvar, 1996; Corey, 1996).

Solution-Focused Therapy

Solution-focused therapy is a story-generating therapy. Story therapies propose that "reality" is merely the current version of a story. Problems exist because people's stories don't empower them to find a solution; the solution is not in the text of the story. In helping people generate new stories, a therapist aids clients to, in essence, write a more productive conclusion. From this perspective, arguments occur because there is a disagreement between stories. When people in dispute can create a new story in tandem, then an impasse can be overcome.

Solution-focused therapy centers around concrete and immediate problem solving. This approach assumes that people have the innate capacity for change, and that given specific tools gained through therapy, change will be swift. An important assumption in solution-focused therapy is that small change is sufficient. If small change occurs as a result of therapy, larger change will naturally follow.

Solution-focused therapists believe that change is a normal life process and that people don't have to delve deeply into why something occurs to change it. What is most important is to instigate change following the desires and interests of the person who wants to change. This theory is based on client needs, but also on the notion that there are alternative perspectives and no one correct way to do things. There are only more and less productive ways to do things. The therapist and client work toward finding productive mechanisms that satisfy client needs.

Techniques for the solution-focused therapist include: *joining*, or building rapport; *exploring exceptions*, identifying what changes have already occurred in order to highlight ways the situation has already changed; *normalizing*, or reconceptualizing the problem to move away from viewing it as a pathology; and, *complimenting*, highlighting the positive and setting the stage for positive reflection. Additionally, specific interventions or exercises are used with all families, regardless of their individual problems. These interventions include: *doing something different; paying attention to what you do when you overcome an urge*; and, *examining what a lot of people would do in your situation* (Kilpatrick & Holland,1995; Newfield, 2000).

Additional Story Generating Therapies

Narrative therapy (Harry Goolishian) uses collaborative conversations to aid people in finding new meanings for their problems. Language and metaphor are utilized as tools for further reflection. Narrative therapists help clients find narratives that support rather than detract from functional and satisfying lives (Becvar & Becvar,1996; Kilpatrick & Holland, 1995).

Reflecting teams (Tom Andersen) are groups of observers who silently listen to a therapy session, then openly reflect on the problem. The therapy participants then in turn reflect on the reflecting teams' observations. The following discussion incorporates the ideas of the reflecting team, redefining and reshaping the problem and possible solutions (Becvar & Becvar, 1996; Kilpatrick & Holland, 1995; Newfield, 2000).

The *Mental Research Institute* (MRI) approach reflects on how dialogue shapes perception. It assumes that reality is malleable and explores how interactive talking helps to co-create reality. MRI uses reframing as an important tool. MRI literature suggests that reframing allows something to fit into two catagories simultaneously. For instance, a rat is in the category of animals with sharp teeth that bite, but also in the category of soft and furry animals. A person's response to a real event will reflect the adopted reframed perspective (Newfield, 1998).

The Physical Environment

The location and environment of mediation can affect the physical and psychological comfort of the participants. In committing to a mediation program, the employer should provide a comfortable space for mediation to occur. The space the employer chooses reveals the credibility of the program. An employer who relegates mediation to a drafty or overheated basement symbolically indicates that mediation is not a priority.

There are some physical details that can seriously detract from the success of mediation. Other features simply make mediation more pleasant. Consider the following factors when choosing a space for mediation.

DEFINING RELATIONSHIPS THROUGH SEATING

Using seating arrangements to gain symbolic power or control is a common practice. For instance, a judge in a courtroom sits elevated behind a large desk to highlight the power of the position. A courtroom audience is set apart from the proceedings by a gate that physically separates participants from nonparticipants. Neither of these barriers physically protects in any significant way, but rather are symbols that help to define relationships.

Seating arrangement in mediation should also be deliberate. In mediation, seating should be used to enhance the concept of equality rather than support an imbalance of power. No participant should be made to feel submissive due to awkward or uncomfortable seating.

ROOM REQUIREMENTS

During the caucusing phase of mediation, either the parties or the mediator moves between rooms. If there are two comfortable rooms, the mediator may choose to travel back and forth so the parties can get acclimated to their space. If two rooms are not available, then the parties must switch.

In addition to the main mediation room, there must be space available for private caucuses. This requires a second meeting room with a table and chairs. If a second room is unavailable, a comfortable and private waiting area should be provided. Privacy protects the anonymity of the participants. Privacy also helps deter gossip or the sharing of misinformation and reduces the emotional stress of the participants.

ROOM SETUP

Mediation is a meeting to conduct business and not group therapy; the physical environment should reflect this. The parties should have a clearly defined space for their belongings. There should always be a table or desk available for taking notes, to physically separate the parties, create a visual barrier, and set the mood.

Mediation rooms and seating should be physically comfortable. People must be able to see and hear well. A table and chairs should be available for everyone, offering easy and complete visual and auditory access to all the participants. There should be adequate light and a comfortable temperature. There should be no outside distractions. A mediation room must be comfortable, private, and quiet.

The mediator should sit between the parties, either at a round table or at the head of a rectangular table. This arrangement allows the mediator to acknowledge participants by turning to each. In fact, all the participants at a mediation should be able to see each other to watch facial and body expressions. People should be seated close enough to see and hear without compromising personal space. People in conflict require more than the culturally standard distance to separate them for comfort.

AMENITIES

Amenities such as access to beverages, access to restrooms, room lighting and temperature can impact stress levels, which affect mediation. None of these elements alone will predict the success or failure of mediation, yet they should not be overlooked. The space an employer chooses for mediation reflects that employer's attitude about the process. An attractive, well-furnished meeting room is ideal. Physical comfort aids psychological comfort. Most important, the mediation room should reflect other important spaces within that organization. The employer must demonstrate that the process has value for the employees to believe it has value.

Access to Comfort

Participation in mediation may lead to feelings of stress or anxiety. Small details can make a difference. It is helpful to have easy access to beverages and restrooms. Dry mouth is common when people are nervous, and some people experience other physical symptoms from stress. A private personal space for retreat can be helpful. In the workplace, the most private space is a restroom; the importance of access to that room is often overlooked.

Lighting

Lighting can affect mood and comfort level. Some people feel uncomfortable in bright fluorescent lighting. A room with soft or natural light that is slightly dim will help relax the participants and may encourage open and honest conversation. It is true that some individuals do not notice room lighting, but for others it can significantly impact mood.

Temperature

Room temperature can be very important as well. If the room temperature is uncomfortable, the meeting will disband sooner. Physical discomfort is also extremely distracting. If people are focusing on their physical needs, they can attend less to the substantive issues of mediation. Overly hot or cold rooms are troublesome. Extreme temperature is uncomfortable. Discomfort promotes stress, which is detrimental to concentration.

DEMEANOR AND SEATING

In organizing seating, the mediator should be aware of the participant's demeanor. In most cases, the participants in mediation act rationally and respectfully. In very rare situations is someone so emotionally distraught or hostile as to pose a threat to the group. Most mediators will never have to contend with a seriously confrontational participant who poses a safety risk. But, to ward off trouble, the mediator should be sensitive to the behavior and attitudes of the parties and seat them accordingly.

Family or group therapists often make it a point to seat certain clients by the door. These people include either the potentially aggressive or overly nervous. Thus, no barrier is presented between a highly agitated person and the exit. Alternatively, if someone is truly out of control, all the other participants may wish to escape. This should not be a cause for paranoia; rather, a mediator should ordinarily be sensitive to body language and demeanor.

SCHEDULING

Time Allocation

Adequate time should be allotted for mediation; the parties should not feel pressured to hurry the session. The amount of time it takes to resolve a conflict through mediation varies and is dependant on many unpredictable factors. The experience, skill, and style of the mediator affect the process length, as do the outlooks of the parties and the specifics of the problem. On average, a workplace mediation requires between one and three hours. Occasionally mediation must be continued across more than one session. Additional mediation may be needed to address issues not considered in the first session.

It is wise to allocate two or three hours for each mediation, with the option of extending the session if needed. The participants must not feel rushed or that they will be penalized for holding a lengthy session. Schedules should be flexible in case a mediation runs long. Policy concerning workplace mediation should be clear and available to the entire workforce.

Scheduling Times

Workplace mediation should be held during working hours and should not be scheduled close to the end of the workday. As part of a commitment to resolving conflict, both the employer and employees must embrace mediation as a job duty. Since mediation has the potential to save time, decrease stress, and dramatically improve the work environment, time in mediation is well spent.

Mediation can be a draining and exhausting activity. Problems addressed during mediation have been a burden for the participants and the prospect of focusing on those issues can be overwhelming. Few people look forward to confrontation and although mediation is not designed to be confrontational, problems are openly discussed and addressed head-on. This experience, while undeniably valuable, is not easy for everyone. All the participants work hard during mediation. Although the relief that comes from resolving disputes is well worth the effort, the process can be difficult. Consequently, it is important to schedule mediation when people are at their best, early in the day.

Employer Benefits. From an employer's perspective, mediation is an excellent tool because resolving disputes increases productivity, decreases downtime spent ruminating over conflict, curbs destructive office gossip, helps build alliances that support group work, and aids organizational morale. Given the potential benefits of mediation for the employer, it would be erroneous to view mediation as merely a generous gesture benefiting the employees. Resolving conflict is an important job responsibility and, as such, should be scheduled as part of the workday.

Worker Benefits. From the perspective of the worker, mediation can help make work less stressful; it aids in building friendships and stronger collegial relationships; it supports productivity, which can lead to promotion and other job benefits; and it can make the work environment more pleasant and satisfying. Despite these benefits, workers are more likely to commit to the process when it occurs during work hours.

ADDRESSING INCONVENIENCES

A mediator should take responsibility for any inconveniences and inadequacies during the process. The parties take cues from the mediator, so mediator behavior will affect the responses of participants. Thus, the mediator can help to shape the session by demonstrating responsible and considerate behavior.

Regardless of how the mediation program is designed, there are bound to be occasions when things do not go as smoothly as planned. It is important that someone take responsibility for these inconveniences. Since the mediator is the available authority figure, the mediator should accept responsibility, even if the annoyances were caused by someone else. The mediator does not have to accept blame, but rather should recognize these inconveniences and offer apologies. Less than satisfactory circumstances that are acknowledged are more tolerable. The mediator tries to mitigate focus on superficial issues, so that conversation does not deteriorate into irrelevant complaining.

Modeling responsible and respectful behavior is very important for the success of mediation. The workplace sometimes fosters a culture where adversity is addressed by griping. Workers often feel powerless and use accusations to empower themselves. Unfortunately, this tactic is usually not very conducive to positive change; it mostly serves to create an unpleasant work environment. The mediator must avoid this trap during mediation. Offering an apology for minor inconveniences helps to relieve tension and demonstrates that it is possible to accept personal responsibility as a show of good faith. The mediator models a healthy way to address common annoyances before they become dramatic events.

GUESTS

In some types of mediation the parties come represented by attorneys. Attorneys are welcome at mediation, but if only one side is represented, the unrepresented party must be given the opportunity to reschedule after securing their own attorney. Occasionally other guests such as union representatives or insurance adjusters attend mediation. Some mediation agreements can only be finalized with these agents present. In this case, with mutual acquiescence, these representatives are welcome.

People acting as witnesses are rarely invited to mediation. The mediation process seeks to avoid courtroom-like testimony. People who may potentially be witnesses in a lawsuit should not attend mediation because there is a risk they will learn confidential information. In the rare instance that a party wishes to have a witness speak on their behalf, approval should be sought from the opposing party.

Within the court system, mediation is likened to a "settlement conference." Consequently, nothing said during mediation can be used in a court proceeding later. This is a worthwhile policy for all mediation. Mediation should be confidential. The parties should not fear that what they reveal will be used to punish them later. Before the mediation begins, the parties and any guests should agree in writing to maintain confidentiality.

If any guests are attending the mediation, they should be seated at the main table as part of the group. People who do not sit at the group table refrain from participation and appear to be interrupting if they do speak. If guests want to attend the session, the opposing party should have the right to over-rule the invitation. Unless mandated by mediation policy, guests are only welcome if all the parties assent.

Mediator Opening Remarks

At the start of mediation the mediator presents an opening statement or opening remarks. The opening remarks serve to set the mood of the session, build rapport, and describe the mediation process. As the leader of a mediation session it is the mediator's job to begin a dialogue. People come to mediation with numerous questions, many of them unarticulated. Since mediation is a new experience for many people, they do not know what questions to ask. Nerves and stress also hinder peoples' ability to clearly identify concerns. In the opening remarks, the mediator should present critical information about the process.

Opening remarks also offer the mediator a chance to gauge the mood of the participants: Are they hostile? Do they appear serious about the process? Do they seem frightened? The demeanor of the participants, which reflects the past relationship, will affect the process. The mediator must contend with attitudes and feelings that may hinder this process. During the mediation session, the mediator attempts to create an environment more conducive to open communication.

Mediators use the opening remarks to help define relationships. Some mediators present themselves as authority figures. Other mediators believe that to maintain self-determination the parties must guide the process. In the clarification of roles the mediator begins to build rapport. Clearly identifying appropriate behavior aims to circumvent the chaos of the past and develop a sense of trust.

Opening remarks also serve an important informational purpose. Opening remarks highlight critical issues about the process and offer the parties an opportunity to generate questions. Mediation is a new experience for most participants who may have preconceptions. An explanation of the agenda, rules, and mediator expectations is needed to shape the process. The parties require adequate direction in order to behave appropriately and experience success.

SETTING THE MOOD

Although mediation is in some respects a traditional meeting to address business concerns, mediation also provides a context for open dialogue. It must not take on the air of a courtroom or workplace evaluation. To assure this, during the opening statement mediators often stress the informality of the process, coupled with the need to display respect.

People come to mediation with fears and hesitation about what will be expected of them. Mediation involves private matters that may have caused pain and confusion in the past. In the workplace, mediation may involve individuals with unbalanced job status and power. There may be concerns about revealing information and how that will affect worklife in the future.

Many mediation participants have already attempted to address their issues and have been thwarted or unsuccessful. They may doubt that mediation will serve a productive purpose and harbor some hostility toward the process. A participant may have come to mediation through pressure from the employer and may resent having to attend. It is also common in workplace mediation for one of the parties to believe there is no problem at all. When this occurs a participant may be unwilling to discuss the matter or unable to acknowledge the concerns of the other person.

A mediator that exhibits an open and generous attitude will help the parties to feel comfortable. Mediators demonstrate empathy and an interest in the problem. The participants will naturally model the attitude and demeanor of the mediator. They will note what is socially appropriate behavior as demonstrated by the mediator. The presentation of opening remarks illustrates how people are expected to behave.

BUILDING RAPPORT

Building rapport simply means developing a relationship. The mediator aims to create an environment in which people feel safe, stress and inhibitions are low, and discussions flow freely without the fear of judgment or reprisal. Opening remarks should focus on strengthening trust while quelling stress and trepidation. The parties will naturally view the mediator as an authority figure. The mediator is the expert on the mediation process and is present to assist with a problem that has yet to be resolved.

Introductions

Introductions are the first phase of the discussion process. The mediator should take this opportunity to notice small details: Where are people sitting? What does their body language reveal? Are they silent or making small talk? Group chatting is a sign that people are relaxed. Notice the mood in the room—a mediator must be keenly aware of details that others might miss.

Consider how to address the parties and how they might respond. Using first names sets a different tone than using surnames. Some people feel more relaxed when on a first-name basis, others are offended at this familiarity. Everyone should be made to feel comfortable.

Ground Rules

Some mediators present guidelines or ground rules for behavior. Ground rules are instructions that guide interaction. Ground rules generally include an admonition about interrupting and quarreling, and a reminder about demonstrating respect. In order to emphasize self-determination, some mediators insist that the parties determine ground rules for themselves. These mediators believe that imposing restrictions would be tantamount to controlling the decision-making process. If a mediator intends to have the parties design ground rules, this should be done after the mediator opening remarks and prior to the participant opening remarks.

Beginning mediators who feel insecure about their own role may wish to set ground rules to gain a personal sense of security. This proactive measure serves to prevent, or to prepare an effective response to, situations temporarily out of control. If the parties know their boundaries, they are more apt to work within them. These boundaries also provide guidance if behavior warrants a reprimand. Ground rules may help the parties feel comfortable and safe. They define the requirements of good faith negotiations, uninterrupted speech, and demonstrated respect and consideration. For those people who have had negative experiences with the opponent previously, ground rules offer the promise of a more positive interaction.

EXPLANATION OF THE PROCESS

After introductions the mediator should offer an explanation of the mediation process. There is standard information that most mediators include in their opening remarks. Mediators may also wish to adapt the opening remarks to fit a personal philosophy and the individual needs of the parties.

The following is an outline of the issues that are generally covered in the opening remarks. Mediators should plan and practice opening remarks and feel free to use written notes during mediation. But opening remarks also offer a time to connect with the parties. Opening remarks are informal but firm. The mediator should avoid presenting a prepared speech.

Opening Remarks Outline

I. Introduction of the mediator and the participants.

II. The mediation process.

    1. Mediation is an opportunity to discuss issues and negotiate openly. Mediation is also an opportunity to learn more about why this conflict occurred in order to prevent future problems.

    2. The goal of mediation is to come to a mutually acceptable and workable resolution. If that is not possible, mediation will help develop a more clear understanding of other perspectives in order to facilitate a future resolution.

III. Role of the mediator.

    1. The mediator is impartial. The mediator does not act as judge and never makes decisions for the parties.

2. The mediator will ask questions to draw out information and may make suggestions. The mediator will help direct the discussion, assisting the parties to evaluate and focus on the important issues.

IV. Role of the participants and ground rules.

1. The participants must discuss all issues openly and in good faith. They must listen carefully and respond respectfully. The participants must be open-minded and creative in considering solutions.

2. The participants may be asked to design ground rules that guide behavior and the mediation process.

V. Confidentiality.

1. The mediator is required to keep all information confidential as explained in the compliance rules. Generally speaking, the mediator will not reveal confidential information to the employer, coworkers, or the court system. All notes taken during mediation are also confidential.

2. The parties are also required to keep all information confidential unless other agreements are made in writing.

3. The mediator and the participants must read and agree to all the workplace mediation rules prior to mediation. The parties must sign an agreement to mediate and a party confidentiality agreement.

VI. Party opening remarks.

1. Party opening remarks provide an opportunity for each side to tell their story without interruption. Each person may speak as long as necessary within a reasonable time limit.

VII. Caucusing.

1. Caucusing is the process in which the mediator speaks with individuals or groups privately. This is a time when issues can be discussed openly and in depth. The mediator will only share information learned during a caucus with the permission of the party.

VIII. Regrouping.

1. Regrouping occurs when all the participants come back together to meet. Negotiations can continue, agreements can be finalized, or plans can be made for the future.

IX. Formalizing agreements.

1. With the assistance of the mediator, the parties complete the memorandum of agreement and the party confidentiality statement.

X. Questions.

1. The mediator asks if there are any questions about the process.

Participant Opening Remarks

After the mediator concludes his or her opening remarks, each side is permitted to tell their story in the presence of all the parties. This is an opportunity for the mediator and the parties to gain a fuller understanding of the problem. It is also a chance to gather information about the participants. The party opening remarks are a summary of the situation from each side's perspective. The parties also highlight any specific issues of particular concern.

TIME LIMITS ON OPENING REMARKS

Some mediators opt for putting time limits on participant opening remarks. But unless there is some external time pressure, there is rarely any need to restrict the participants. Participants rarely disrupt the process with unreasonably long statements. If a party does speak for an exceptionally long time or attempts to dominate the process, the mediator can use subtle prompts to signal the speaker.

Interjecting with a question disrupts the speaker's train of thought and is a useful way to break a pattern without appearing controlling. Questions direct a person toward a specific goal. The mediator also can comment that the position being expressed is understood. Useful prompts include: "I think you have done a good job of explaining the situation"; "I have a good idea of what is going on from your perspective"; "If you have nothing else to add, would you mind if we hear from the other party now?" Here, the mediator takes an affirmative step to guide the process without an appearance of force. A mediator must take heed—when halting a speaker there is a risk that some important information will be preempted.

SPEAKING ORDER

The mediator usually determines which party will speak first. Some mediators use an objective approach—for instance, beginning on the left side of the room. Other mediators begin with the side they believe will tell the logical beginning of the story, perhaps the party who initiated mediation. It is not particularly important who starts the process, but it is very important that all the participants feel they are treated equally. A simple explanation of why the choice was made should satisfy the participants.

INITIATING DIALOGUE

In most instances people will begin their stories with little prompting. If one side appears stuck or denies that there is a problem, the mediator can allow the opponent to proceed. Since there is bound to be some contention between the two perspectives, this should help to begin a dialogue.

To initiate dialogue the mediator can also use simple prompts, such as "Tell us about the situation" or "What has happened here?" These are simply cues that it is time to begin telling the story. The person sharing will usually describe the situation in sufficient detail to generate a conversation. It is still appropriate for the mediator to interject questions if additional prompting is required or an important point needs clarification.

UNINTERRUPTED SPEECH

Opening remarks are generally made without interruption. The opportunity for uninterrupted speech serves several purposes. First, it allows a person to speak without distraction and to focus on important issues without being led astray. Also, opening remarks are an important opportunity to vent concerns directly to the opponent, in the presence of a nonthreatening mediator. During this speech the mediator models appropriate conduct by displaying silent attention.

Occasionally the participants begin to argue back and forth during opening remarks. Although debate often serves an important function in mediation, argument tends to make people focus on their next point rather than listen attentively to the speaker. The opening remarks are a time to listen and be heard. The mediator should encourage full attention.

Opening remarks present an extremely important learning opportunity. This may be the first conversation in which energy is focused on listening. Since conflict is frequently spurred by miscommunication and misunderstanding, hearing what the other person has to say is an important step toward resolving the dispute.

Listening to a person speak also provides an opportunity to examine patterns of speech, body language, the focus of concerns, and emotional demeanor. These are important indicators of how the mediation will progress. There is a great deal to learn from what a person has to say and how they say it. An opponent is often unaware of the passion and distress revealed during opening remarks. This first opportunity to speak freely and uninterrupted is cathartic and offers surprises.

GROUP DISCUSSION VERSUS
PRIVATE CAUCUS

After each party has had ample time to present opening remarks, the mediator may open the floor for discussion. Many mediators believe that full-group discussion is necessary to help the parties learn to communicate more effectively. Other mediators see the private caucus as an effective way to address hidden issues hindering effective communication. After the opening remarks, the mediator guides the parties to either a group discussion or a private meeting.

Most mediators adopt a general protocol, but also remain flexible and take cues from the parties. It is wise for a beginning mediator to have a strategy. Entering mediation without a plan can lead to confusion. Uncertainty expressed by the mediator may be uncomfortable for the parties. Adaptability is not analogous to indecisiveness. It is important that the mediator appear confident and directed.

A group discussion may flow naturally without prompting, or the mediator may need to intervene. Some participants will independently engage in conversation but others will sit awkwardly in silence. The mediator can direct communication by summarizing, rephrasing, and asking questions. If conversation becomes clearly unproductive because of silence or destructive bickering, the mediator may commence private caucusing.

The mediator should follow the direction of the parties, but should not permit a session to become out of control. The parties are unlikely to request a private caucus if one is not offered. A fruitless or painful group discussion may destroy mediation if the mediator does not intervene. The parties will invariably, and gratefully, follow the mediator's lead in these situations.

The most productive approach for many mediators is to begin private caucusing soon after opening remarks, unless it is apparent that the parties will benefit from further group discussion. The parties need an opportunity to express their concerns and feelings without the opposing side passing judgment. People must be permitted to vent frustrations without the fear of reprimand. Such an environment must be created by the mediator. There is never a guarantee that opposing parties will tolerate free expression in a group setting. The only way to assure complete liberty of speech is to hold discussions privately.

Opening remarks present an opportunity for the mediator to assess the issues and temperament of the participants. From these remarks, the mediator will have a sense of whether the parties will be forthcoming in a group session. If the parties indicate through their demeanor that group discussion will be fruitful, certainly hold a group session. The parties should be practicing productive communication; to accomplish this they must interact. Group interaction is a critical part of mediation and should not be ignored. It should, however, be postponed if the goals of the group meeting cannot initially be met.

Many mediators agree that the parties are more at ease and forthcoming during the caucus than in a group session. Caucusing permits the mediator to learn about the parties and strategically plan for a fruitful group discussion later on. Group discussion should not mimic the chaotic communication the parties previously experienced. Mediation must offer something different. If mediation is merely a repeat of the difficulty already experienced, change is unlikely. After private caucuses, when the critical issues have been identified and the parties are freed of pent-up feelings, then a productive group meeting is more likely.

STRATEGIC PLANNING

Through opening remarks the mediator gains an understanding of the participants and begins to plan a strategy for the session. Interventions should be designed to anticipate parties' responses. The mediator does not work to satisfy a predetermined agenda, but does attempt to predict patterns. The mediator aims to remain a step ahead, working to minimize any surprises that can overwhelm the process.

Caucusing

A caucus is a private meeting with the mediator. Most mediators divide the mediation session into group meetings and private caucuses. The first group meeting begins with the mediator and participant opening remarks. This meeting is often followed by private caucusing. Whether or not the mediator should initiate a caucus, and how the mediator shares information learned during a caucus, is perhaps the most controversial aspect of the mediation process. Caucusing has both benefits and drawbacks.

CAUCUSING VERSUS FULL-GROUP SESSIONS

The Caucus

Some mediators believe that caucusing is the heart of the mediation process and the primary opportunity to delve deeply into the issues and feelings surrounding the conflict. Conflict is in part created because of behavior patterns that have become ingrained in the relationship that the parties are unable or unwilling to transform on their own. For the dynamics of the relationship to change, independent work is necessary to alter perceptions that hinder productive communication. The caucus offers the parties an opportunity to investigate the problem in a judgment-free environment where possibilities can be explored without the risk of losing face or risking reprisal. After the issues have been examined in a nonthreatening arena, the parties can be freed from the burden of their history and begin to change thinking and behavior.

In situations in which the problem is less emotionally focused, the caucus still offers many of the same benefits: the opportunity to speak freely about negotiation positions, the desired outcomes, and possible risks and rewards of settlement. Business-oriented negotiations often include private information that is valuable to the settlement process, but cannot be shared openly with the opposing side. The mediator and a party can discuss in confidence the pros and cons of revealing pertinent private information and can design strategies for resolving the conflict without sharing information that might be detrimental. Parties also hold information that, while not inherently private, may serve to exacerbate the conflict rather than resolve it. In a private caucus the mediator can work with the party to tailor communication about this information so it will not inflame the opponent.

Full-Group Discussion

Alternatively, some mediators feel just as strongly that caucusing should be avoided, particularly in disputes that are emotionally based or involve a continuing relationship. This style of mediation is centered around full-group discussions. One of the fundamental purposes of mediation, and a great benefit of the process, is that mediation encourages people to speak openly to each other and enhances interpersonal and communication skills. It is antithetical to the purpose of mediation to separate the parties into private meetings where they cannot learn information firsthand. The human skills needed for productive intercommunication are best learned through live interaction, which can only be obtained in a group.

In group meetings the mediator acts as a facilitator but not as an intermediary. In caucusing, the information shared with the opposing side is filtered through the mediator's personal perceptions and is altered to be more palatable. Advocates of the full-group process argue that caucusing does nothing to build skills for future interaction, when the mediator is not present to intervene. They suggest that the problems that are avoided with caucusing are exactly the problems that most need to be addressed.

The Impact of Conflict

Conflict often results from miscommunication or lack of communication. Many people lack awareness of how their behavior affects other people. When causing others distress, they are oblivious to their influence. They do not intend to cause harm, but lack the sensitivity to recognize their effect or repair the damage. In addition, many people do not verbalize the distress they feel and take no apparent action to resolve their confusion. There is an expectation that the person responsible for the pain should initiate a resolution. This is unrealistic since that person is often not even aware of the trouble. Nonetheless, it appears an extremely common social problem. From all sides there is lack of insight and poor communication that feeds conflict and unrealistic and unfounded negative perceptions of other people.

The goal is to gain a keener insight into how interaction affects other people. When actions are conscientious and deliberate, productive behavior can be substituted to prevent conflict. This is relevant to both interpersonal and business relationships. Since all interaction has an emotional component there is always a risk of damaging relationships when behavior results in confusion. Even in interaction that is not emotion-based, people should seek to find the most productive ways of sharing information and building alliances. Some mediators believe that working in a group is the most efficient and realistic means to attain these goals.

Choosing a Method

Most mediators would agree that working in a group can be more difficult and more volatile. People involved in mediation have not yet learned to properly address their conflict. This may lead to some hostility and thus reservations about open dialogue. In a group meeting there is more likely to be bickering or other displays of destructive emotion. There is a threat that opposing parties may react in a callous manner, not conducive to resolution. This may cause even greater tension between the parties.

Some chaos during the mediation process is to be expected and is even necessary for developing empathy and healing. It is healthy for the parties to be exposed to each others' feelings and ideas, even if these expressions are distasteful or uncomfortable. It is in working through difficulty, with the assistance of the mediator, that the parties can learn more satisfying and productive means of interaction.

Other mediators counter this argument and claim that working through problems in a group is less effective. If the parties could resolve the conflict togther, they already would have done so. An important difference is that the conflict resolution process now includes a mediator, a person with more highly developed skills to work though the confusion. The parties are no longer alone in the resolution process; they now have a competent, caring, and skilled guide.

The theory behind full-group mediation is sound, and perhaps mediations that are successful as a result of this method do promise stronger long-term relationships. There is little, if any, empirical evidence to promote one method over another. Belief in either theory stems mostly from personal perception and experience. Both methods appear satisfactory for those mediators who use them.

There may, however, be serious concerns for inexperienced mediators employing full-group mediation. It is very likely that there will be greater turmoil when the parties are required to work together. Also, the parties may withhold vital information when there is no private and confidential arena for sharing. Unless the mediator has highly advanced counseling skills, it is not recommended that the beginning mediator employ the full-group mediation strategy. Rather, the mediator should divide into caucus groups directly after the opening remarks or when the group discussion becomes unproductive.

ADOPTING THE CAUCUSING APPROACH

For a mediator who does choose to caucus, the caucus is the heart of mediation. It is where the parties reveal their secrets and the negotiations start. The mood of the mediation changes when caucusing begins. As soon as the private session commences, the participants relax and become more open. A sense of pressure is clearly removed when the parties are alone with the mediator. There is no longer a need to perform, harbor painful feelings, or shelter secret information. Invariably, the parties look forward to expressing themselves without self-protection and the caucus is their first opportunity to do this.

In some mediations there are additional people involved besides the two parties. For instance, lawyers or union representatives are sometimes present at mediation. Private caucuses can be held with these people as well. Caucuses can be useful for any individual or group who may have private information to share. While there are usually two official sides to a conflict, individuals on the same side may have differing perspectives or unique information to share. A mediator may wish to meet with each individual separately so there is less pressure to conform to the position of the group. Within sides, personal views may differ. If a lawyer or other representative is present, it can be helpful to talk with this representative alone. Representatives sometimes hold back ideas or issues from their own clients for the sake of maintaining that relationship.

There may be some hesitation when a mediator suggests breaking up sides for private caucusing. Revelations learned by the mediator in a caucus remain a mystery to the other participants. If there are secrets that certain individuals do not want revealed, private caucuses can be a threat. There is no control over what other people will say in the caucus. Even people on the same side of a dispute sometimes reveal conflicting attitudes. If there seems to be hesitation, the mediator should reassure the participants of the confidentiality commitment. And never insist on individual caucusing if members of the group are unsure. A mediator should never risk a break in trust that might destroy the mediation.

Discussion during a caucus usually flows extremely easily. A simple prompt, such as "So what else would you like to tell me?", should be sufficient to motivate discussion. The mediator may wish to begin the discussion by asking a specific question. This technique can be used if there is an outstanding issue in the mediator's mind or if the party is reluctant to initiate dialogue. If a party seems overly hesitant, reiterating the confidentiality promise often relieves fears.

Although participants usually speak freely during a caucus, ambivalence about revealing a particular piece of information may exist. Despite this ambivalence, the mediator is often given some indication that this information exists. This is a sign that the person wishes to divulge the information but is for some reason reluctant. This reluctance is combated with developing trust. A mediator should not pressure the parties to express private matters, but should reassure them. The mediator may choose to redirect a person if they seem to be stuck ruminating over whether to express a secret. As long as the process continues comfortably, the mediator can revisit the issue at a later time and the party will invariably share the secret. Participants want to speak openly and will do so if they feel safe.

The caucusing process requires that the mediator travel back and forth between the private meetings. During this time the mediator gathers information and shifts through the complexities of the problem. This process will continue as long as it is productive. A mediator may move back and forth between the parties a dozen times. With each transition the issues are narrowed and focus is placed on the elements that can be negotiated. The parties are also expressing their concerns and feelings, dismantling barriers that prevent resolution. At any point during the caucusing process the mediator may bring the parties back together for a group meeting. Depending on the nature of the dispute and the attitudes of the parties, the details of an agreement may or may not be developed with the parties in the same room.

MEDIATOR ROLE

The role of the mediator is somewhat different during caucusing than during group meetings. This is due to the private and confidential nature of the caucus. During a group meeting all information is public knowledge. The mediator's role is primarily that of facilitator. The mediator asks questions, reframes, and rephrases, but the mediator has less control in affecting the dynamics of the group.

During caucusing, the mediator can have real influence and power over what each side learns about the other, and their interpretation of information. During caucusing the mediator takes significant personal responsibility for the resolution process and the outcome of the case. This is one reason some mediators are less comfortable with the caucusing process. A mediator always walks a fine line between giving assistance and taking control.

During caucusing the mediator must be extremely cognizant of what information is being shared between the caucus rooms and how it is being reinterpreted. The mediator must be cautious when translating or reframing parties' statements. A mediator who inadvertently misleads the parties risks seriously derailing the negotiations and hurting the future relationship of the parties. Since the parties are not present to hear what the mediator says in each room, the mediator must self-monitor.

Despite the mediator's potential influence on the dynamics of the process, there is little a mediator can do to persuade a person to do something distasteful, uncomfortable, or improper. The parties will not make agreements that they do not wish to make, although sometimes they do make agreements they are unable to keep. When gauging the mediator's influence over the parties, concern should not be placed primarily on how final resolutions are affected, but on how mischaracterization of a party's feelings will influence future interpersonal dynamics. Although the parties will probably not make agreements that offend their sensibilities, in a sincere attempt to bring them together for resolution, the mediator can easily distort ongoing relationships by misrepresenting the perceptions and feelings of the parties.

Illustration of Mediator Influence

An illustration of this predicament would be the following: One of the parties, the supervisor of the opponent party, tells the mediator during a private caucus that this subordinate worker has been slacking off on the job. The supervisor believes that this worker's problem stems from trouble at home.

There is a rumor that the worker is in the process of getting divorced. The supervisor acknowledges that he is sympathetic to this difficult personal dilemma, but cannot tolerate lazy and irresponsible work habits. The mediator, not wanting to inflame the worker, particularly in light of his home difficulties, tells him that the supervisor is sympathetic to his personal problem and hopes that it will not affect work performance.

The mediator aims to defuse any hostility and bring these people closer so they can agree on terms for a resolution. The mediator also wants to dissuade the parties from harboring bad feelings, in order to strengthen the future relationship. The problem is that the mediator misrepresented the supervisor's true message in an attempt to make the information palatable. The most important piece of information was that the work habits must change. The fact the supervisor was also sympathetic could be helpful to the relationship, but does not entirely guide the supervisor's judgment.

After coming to an agreement about tasks that must be completed, the mediation ends. Two weeks later the worker, thinking the supervisor will be even more understanding, neglects his work to a greater extent. The supervisor is even more angered, feeling that the agreement has been breached. The worker then becomes angry and hurt, feeling that the supervisor lied and manipulated during the mediation by demonstrating insincere sympathy.

Although the mediator does want to filter information in a way that supports stronger relationships, the mediator must be careful that both the information and sentiment are accurately portrayed. To assure this, the mediator uses a number of techniques. Reframing and rephrasing are used to express empathy for the ideas and feelings of the parties and also to check the accuracy of the mediator's interpretations. Before moving from one caucus group to another, the mediator should review with the party what is to be shared and how to share it. This is not a suggestion that the mediator prepare a speech, but that the mediator should clarify with the participant that there is a meeting of the minds.

Mediator Responsibilities

In caucusing, the mediator has several important responsibilities. First, the mediator is a keen and empathetic listener. The mediator offers an opportunity for the parties to express information and feelings without judgment. The mediator should refrain from making any evaluations or posing challenging questions, at least until trust is evident. The mediator has an open ear. During the initial explanation of the problem the mediator can interject using rephrasing techniques to demonstrate understanding.

The manner in which the mediator expresses him or herself will depend on the parties' needs and the circumstances of the case. The mediator will respond differently to an emotional response than to more clinical accounts of the problem. Not all parties will openly express emotion; not all cases reveal overtly emotional issues. Whether the tenor of the session is more personal or more business-oriented, the mediator must still demonstrate respect, consideration, empathy, and understanding of the problem.

TECHNIQUES

Asking Questions

After the party has described the situation sufficiently, the mediator can begin to ask questions. Questions posed by the mediator are very important to the mediation process. Asking questions shows that the mediator is listening and desires to fully understand the problem. Also, asking questions is an excellent way to challenge the perceptions held by the parties, without imposing unwanted ideas or appearing threatening. A question can present a new idea or a new interpretation of a problem without stating that this new interpretation is correct, but merely something to consider. In asking questions the mediator introduces a buffer because a question is not a conclusion and there is no harm done if the participant answers the question in a manner that discredits the idea. Unlike suggestions or advice, questions are inquisitive rather than directive. Yet questions can be more effective for presenting ideas than a more direct approach, which may be taken as an affront to the beliefs of the party.

A useful mediator tool is to pose the same question to both sides or to ask one party what they suspect the other party thinks or feels about an issue. This is an excellent way to assist the parties in exploring the perspective of the other side, without juxtaposing mutually contradictory interpretations. Asking the parties to reflect on each other's thoughts can only be accomplished during a caucus. If this technique is used in a group session, there is a high probability that the parties will bicker, increasing hostility. Invariably the language used by one party to explain the thoughts of another will not sound "right." This will only escalate conflict.

Another technique is to ask one party to rephrase the statement of an opponent during a group meeting, to mirror the statement. This does not require the depth of reflection required in interpreting suspected thoughts. Mirroring is more like mimicking and may be useful to bring understanding or at least some agreement to the nature of the problem. However, it has less impact than speculating in depth.

Generating Questions. The mediator may also ask for advice on questions to pose to the other side. This leads the parties to more fully question their own ideas, confusions, and concerns. It also facilitates exploring alternative perceptions. In developing questions, the participants will contemplate their opponent's answers to those questions. The assumptions made about the answers may or may not be correct; either way, it is a learning experience. When the mediator then poses these questions to the opponent, it is a clue as to the thinking of the question generator.

During a group session, the mediator can ask: "Do you have any questions for the other side?", but there is really no opportunity in this interaction for serious contemplation. The response is usually "no," or a repetition of some dysfunctional interaction, perhaps a round of bickering. Generating questions with the mediator in private has a completely different dynamic. A discussion or debate can occur that does not threaten the relationship or a potential resolution. Questions can be composed that the parties were afraid to ask or were unable to conceive because the conflict blocked clear and expansive thought. Well-designed and thoughtful questions generated by the parties themselves offer great insight into the thinking of both sides, through the answers to the questions and the questions themselves.

Reflecting

Reflecting is a strategy similar to generating questions. The mediator can ask one party to make suggestions about how to handle the caucus with the other side. Together the mediator and the participant can explore assumptions about how the other party will behave and what will be the most effective techniques for generating resolution. Having one party speculate about the behavior of another assists them to predict future behavior that can be applied to the workplace. An important key to preventing and resolving conflict is learning to react in a consciously directed manner. Not all people respond positively to the same cues. Developing a battery of individually tailored strategies for dealing with particular people is very valuable for preventing conflict.

Reflecting on the patterns of thoughts, feelings, and actions of other people is an exercise sometimes overlooked. Many people reflect on their own thoughts, feelings, and actions, but neglect to consider those of other people. Examining the response patterns of oneself and of others is invaluable for predicting and preparing for future interactions. It also helps in building empathy and appreciation for other people, which is always helpful for avoiding conflict.

Reframing

Reframing is another technique that can be used during caucusing. Reframing includes translating or redefining. In reframing, the content of the message is communicated, but the language is changed in such a way that the spirit or feeling is altered. By slightly altering a statement, reframing assists the parties to reconceptualize their ideas, thus redefining the problem and the potential solutions.

All people view the world and interactions through a personal filter that is shaped by many factors, such as individual upbringing, personalities, and life experiences. No two people have identical views. Even when people agree about matters, it is difficult for any two people to have a true meeting of the minds, because there is a subjective reality that is inherently impossible to communicate. This leads people to design rules and procedures that can be mutually agreed on and that guide outward behavior. Even so, interpretations and responses to these rules can differ.

The personal interpretation of "truth" is also a subjective phenomenon. Two people can have very different perspectives on the truth in any given situation. Even the "facts" of particular situations are often disputed. Since descriptions of events are subjective, they can change and are never stagnant. People reevaluate their lives and surroundings at every moment. Life is affected by a constant reexamining of self and the outside world. Learning is a progression of the conscious interpretation of truth. Therefore, as people learn more about a problem, they redefine the problem to fit a new and updated understanding of the truth.

In other words, life is a story. The ending or any piece in between can be altered with a small change in the details. Here is an example: when a person is in the heat of anger, that individual maintains very strong and often overwhelming ideas and feelings on the subject that makes them angry. This is the time when people often step back and wait. They refrain from actively addressing the problem or confronting the person until they are able to "gain perspective." After taking some time and ruminating over the circumstances, ideas and feelings about the problem change. Sometimes anger or frustration subsides and more clarity is gained. It is not that this newfound perspective on the problem is more right or true, but it is often more conducive to communication, resolution, and ultimately sane living.

In a final evaluation, a person may determine that the initial interpretation of events was accurate and anger was warranted, but this is one person's perspective. Despite the rightness of a particular perspective, tools are employed to change personal perspectives to reflect individual needs. Critical or rational thinking is employed to change the story and create a new story that permits more functional interaction.

The new story then becomes the truth. This is an altered truth, but truth nonetheless. The details have been changed in hopes of changing the outcome. This reflects subjective reality, and is fundamentally important for resolving problems. Simply put, people change their lives by changing their stories. This is the purpose of reframing.

When the mediator reframes statements for the participants, the mediator presents a subtle reinterpretation of the details. This is not an attempt to manipulate the person into believing something different, and it is not an imposition of the mediator's own perspective. Rather, reframing presents a new example, a slightly altered way of perceiving the same issues. A reframe is not a demand or even a suggestion, just an alternative possibility that the participant is free to accept, reject, or alter in a new way.

During a conversation each person reflects on what the other says. In responding to someone's ideas, those ideas are filtered though a personal thought process. The response, a reinterpretation encompassing their ideas, in part, but not in whole, is a reframe. Listening to a statement and then responding with "I understand, but what about——," is a reframing. Reframing is very close to rephrasing, "I understand, you are saying——," but with a slight but deliberate alteration. The alteration can have a significant effect on the impact and intent of the idea. It changes the story. But when a mediator reframes, it is offered as a possibility, less than a suggestion, simply an option. Even the mediator does not know if the reframed idea is a good one. It is a mutual inquiry with the party in search of a more effective way to view the problem.

Neutrality

During the caucus the mediator becomes the bearer of information. The mediator acts as an intermediary between the parties. When the mediator adopts caucusing in place of a group session, the mediator becomes responsibile for shuttling information back and forth between the parties. The mediator makes determinations about what will and will not be revealed, although still respecting the wishes and intentions of the parties.

The mediator should note a contradiction in the job responsibilities. The mediator must be true to the messages presented by the parties. The mediator must reflect accurately both the content and intent of the information. But the mediator may also reframe these messages in order to make the information more palatable and help bring the parties together. These requirements conflict, which makes the job of a mediator difficult.

In every mediation session the mediator is faced with a challenge: to actively assist the parties in making change without imposing notions that are unwanted or unauthorized. The most simple way to address this problem is with candor. Before leaving one caucus room, the mediator should review all the information that will be shared. Both the content and the tenor or intent should be noted. The parties should have a clear picture of what will be revealed to the other side. However, the mediator and the parties must accept that the mediator does have influence on the process. This is a sensitive subject in the field of mediation; how can the mediator be completely impartial as the process unfolds?

It is difficult to define neutrality or impartiality as it applies to mediation. The mediator does not want to disrupt the process. But absolute neutrality would require that the mediator refrain from interjecting or intervening, perhaps defeating the purpose of commissioning a mediator. Most mediators claim to be neutral or impartial, yet there is disagreement as to how impartiality is to be maintained. It is difficult to preserve complete neutrality while taking affirmative steps to assist.

The dilemma compels the mediator to seek interventions that will not threaten the self-determination of the parties, or their right to view issues subjectively and to resolve conflict to their personal satisfaction. It is essential that mediators maintain a heightened sensitivity to their own actions. Mediators should be cautious and must never neglect to address even small details with the parties. Mediators, like all people, have preconceptions, independent ideas, and even prejudices. The parties do understand this and expect mediation to be a shared inquiry and a group challenge. If a situation arises in which a mediator becomes aware of an error in his or her own judgment, the mediator should be forthright in revealing it. An open discussion of this potential mistake is an opportunity to model humility and a desire to understand.

Asking Questions

An essential task of the mediator is to ask questions. The most obvious purpose of asking questions is to elicit information. At the start of mediation the mediator knows little or nothing about the case. Surprisingly, the parties frequently know little about the case. Often there is so much confusion surrounding the problem that the focus of the argument is not clear. Also, the perspectives of the parties may be so divergent that the conflict consists of entirely different issues for the parties.

Since the mediator is the only unbiased person present, it is incumbent on the mediator to assist the parties in examining previously unidentified nuances of the problem. In listening to the opening remarks, the mediator will gain a sense of where personal focus lies, where parties diverge, where there is confusion, and where there is simply a lack of information. The people involved in the dispute may be so entrenched in their own positions and perspectives that they are unable to recognize personal limitations.

By asking questions, the mediator focuses the controversy, magnifying critical issues and shading the less pertinent concerns. Since it is not the job of the mediator to dictate the flow of a meeting, questioning the parties helps reveal their priorities in the natural course of discussion. The mediator asks questions that aid in directing the conversation, but the parties, through their answers, have control over what is revealed, when it is revealed, and how.

OPEN-ENDED QUESTIONS

Questions by the mediator can also serve additional functions. Questions can be a catalyst for discussion. The mediator presents a simple point or observation, "Is that issue a concern for you?" and the parties, responding to the cue, discuss the issue in more depth. The majority of questions posed by the mediator will be formed as open-ended questions. The question itself does not suggest an answer. Open-ended questions do not steer toward an answer. The person responding does not sense a particular answer is expected—rather, the question expresses a general curiosity about the topic.

Perhaps the most typical, or stereotypical, open-ended question is: "How do you feel about that?" Variations on this question might include, "What do you think about that?" "Why do you think that is happening?" "What would you like to have happen?" or any other adaptation of a broad question that prompts further thought.

Open-ended questions are not likely to impose the mediator's perceptions on the discussion. Open-ended questions encourage the participants to reflect on their individual concerns while offering some direction. Open-ended questions are helpful to combat a number of obstacles that may arise during mediation. Some mediation participants may feel overwhelmed. Others are not comfortable with probing conversation. Still others may find themselves stuck or unable to focus. Immobility stemming from any cause will make a lull in the conversation worse by exacerbating tension. Open-ended questions advance gentle guidance for participants who lack focus.

Alternatively, some people tend to speak in a stream-of-consciousness fashion. They do not have trouble communicating ideas and feelings, but do have difficulty pinpointing the most significant concerns. Although the mediator does not want to subvert a conversation, and much valuable information can be learned from this type of rambling speech, there are times when offering guidance can be helpful. While open-ended questions do sometimes elicit stream-of-consciousness responses, for a person who has begun to ramble, additional open-ended questions can introduce a structure without appearing controlling.

CLOSED-ENDED QUESTIONS

Closed-ended questions direct a person to a yes-or-no answer or a short concise reply. Closed-ended questions do not evoke deep consideration or an in-depth exploration of ideas. They are primarily used when a mediator is seeking specific information. There are instances when closed-ended questions are appropriate in mediation—for instance, to confirm factual data.

Examples of useful closed-ended questions include: "What is your job description?" or "How many years have you worked with Mr. Smith?" If the mediator is interested in knowing how the participant feels about the relationship with Mr. Smith, than a closed-ended question is a poor choice. If the mediator asks: "Is your relationship with Mr. Smith good?" the answer to this question will likely be either "yes" or "no." A better way to evoke this information would be with an open-ended request: "Tell me about your relationship with Mr. Smith."

If the participant finds it difficult to focus on a broad question, a closed-ended question may be used as a catalyst for further discussion. The interaction might proceed as follows: "It seems as if the arguments between you and Mr. Smith are causing difficulties at work." "Yes, I guess that is true." "Would it be fair to say that these arguments are affecting your productivity at work?" "Yes, I don't think I am accomplishing as much as I would like to." "Can you describe to me some of the arguments the two of you have had, and could you give me examples of how these arguments have affected your work?" The participant is led with closed-ended questions to focus on a particular problem. Once the problem is identified, open-ended questions are asked, presenting an opportunity to elaborate.

PROBING QUESTIONS

Another form of question that may be used by the mediator is the probing question. A probing question is different from a closed-ended question. A closed-ended question leads a person to a specific answer, although it does not assume what the answer will be. The answer to a closed-ended question may be either "yes" or "no," but the question itself does not presuppose which of those responses the question will elicit. A probing question is also different from an open-ended question. Open-ended questions are broad prompts used as a catalyst for discussion. The direction a person takes with an open-ended question is totally unpredictable. The focus of the answer is determined by the person answering the question.

The probing question is less neutral than either the open or closed-ended question. When a mediator asks a probing question, he or she has some particular agenda in mind, a preconceived idea of how the party should interpret an issue or what direction the answer should take. Probing questions are most often employed when the mediator has a sense that an issue is important, but the party has not independently explored the topic. The mediator can use a probing question to suggest that the issue be further examined. To avoid being overly directive, probing questions can be presented in a fashion that expresses curiosity.

Having an unbiased viewpoint, the mediator is able to recognize important issues that have been overlooked or hidden. A mediator can have a keen sense of the dynamics fueling the conflict and the possible resolutions. But because the parties reap the most benefit when they reach their own revelations, the mediator will avoid subjecting the parties to proclamations. The mediator must find a tool to share this insight without imposing. Probing questions offer the mediator an opportunity to lead the parties in a general direction, but still allow the parties to reject the notions in a nonconfrontational manner. The parties usually have enough autonomy to reject or redirect a probing question through their response without having to directly oppose the mediator.

Probing questions are often prefaced with an equivocal statement: "I wonder if this is a possibility," "Have you considered," or "From what you told me, I have this idea." Probing questions then direct the party to consider a specific idea. "Have you considered that your arguments with Mr. Smith might be affecting his productivity as well? How do you suspect that affects the way he treats you?" Here a probing question suggests the possibility that there is an alternative perspective. By helping to promote empathy, this line of questioning may lead the parties to a better understanding of each other's predicaments and to finding a middle ground.

Another example of a probing question is: "From what you have told me I see that you are very frustrated with your supervisor; you sense that her treatment of you is unfair and biased. You told me that she doesn't like you, but, from everything you said, you sound like a conscientious and productive worker. Can you think of any reasons she might have misjudged you?"

This question employs a number of tools. Rephrasing and reframing helps to build trust and an understanding between the mediator and the party. The mediator then asks a probing question that is phrased in a nonthreatening way. Although stated in a tactful manner, this question suggests the possibility that there is another rational interpretation of the situation. The mediator could never say: "What did you do to make your supervisor so mad?" The party would be hurt and offended. The questioning must suggest possible alternatives without causing anger, frustration, humiliation, or fear.

The mediator does not want to alienate or frustrate the parties to the point where discussion is no longer productive. But the mediator can use probing questions to challenge the preconceptions of the participants. In coming to mediation, the parties understand that resolving conflict is difficult work and not always comfortable. They look to the mediator for an expanded view of the problem, which sometimes reveals ideas that are new and awkward. However, any challenge presented by the mediator must never come across as a condemnation. A challenge should imply respect for the capacity to live up to the challenge. A mediator who gently pushes the parties toward a novel examination conveys that their problems are worth the effort of an intellectual and emotional struggle.

CROSS-EXAMINATION

While it is appropriate to impose some structure on the conversation, the mediator must be cautious not to take on an authoritarian role. The most common mistake made by mediators, even experienced ones, is to "cross-examine" the parties. The tendency to ask questions for which the answers are implicit is common. But in mediation this practice can be very destructive. Imposing assumptions onto the parties strips them of their self-determination, their right to a personal and independent assessment of the problem.

But perhaps the most important reason not to lead the parties to particular conclusions is that it is not fruitful in the long run. An authoritarian mediator may be very successful at reaching settlements, but once that mediator is removed from the relationship, the parties are subject to an agreement they did not freely design. This leads to the inevitable failure of the agreement. In retrospect, the parties may begin to resent the actions of the mediator and refrain from performing the agreed on tasks. A settlement that the parties cannot or will not maintain only exacerbates the problem.

QUESTIONING MISTAKES

The failure of mediation due to inappropriate interference by a mediator may be more damaging than having had no mediation at all. Although few mediators intentionally abuse their power, many mediators do find it difficult to locate the appropriate balance between presenting possibilities and controlling. There are common mistakes that mediators make in asking questions. Sometimes the mistake is with the wording of the question and sometimes in the tone of voice. With an accusatory tone of voice the mediator can effectively put a party on the defensive.

Examples of potentially disruptive phrases include: "You make no sense"; "You shouldn't feel that way"; "I want to know why you did that"; "What is your problem?" In making these statements, the mediator is not intending to threaten or intimidate, but is implying an accusation. These comments force the participant into a defensive rather than reflective mode of thinking. The shift in control empowers the mediator and disempowers the parties. Mediators do make unintentional but natural mistakes. In many aspects of life people must give orders and present thoughts with an air of authority. Frequently the mediator is not even aware that he or she is threatening or accusatory.

OPINIONS AND ADVICE

As the mediation progresses, the parties will want stronger input. A point may be reached during mediation when enough trust has been built that the mediator can safely critique a perspective. If the party clearly feels comfortable, and requests that the mediator make conclusive observations, then at the mediator's discretion he or she may express opinions or offer advice.

Some mediators have a strict policy against this practice. Offering advice, even when requested, can be problematic. Even when advice is freely accepted, people are often reluctant to follow it. In fact, advice is frequently resented and interpreted as criticism. In many instances it is. Unsolicited advice is even more detrimental because it tends to annoy and frustrate. Advice is often rejected in part because the recommendation is difficult to perform.

Advice regularly reflects common sense, and the person with the problem has already considered it and failed. When someone presents advice as an easy answer, "Why don't you just do——" the person being given the advice feels belittled. If the person could "just do" something, they would. Presenting an idea in this fashion suggests that the person is a failure and is unable to accomplish a task that anyone else could "just do." Whether or not others can "just do" something is irrelevant to that particular person's predicament.

If a mediator does offer advice, it should always be sincere and tactful. It is not the mediator's job to teach the participants a lesson. The mediator should always be careful not to make the parties feel foolish. Advice must come across as thoughtful and considerate, not intended to scold or humiliate. Also, the mediator must assure the parties that they are not required to take the advice; that this advice merely presents one option.

Despite the mediator's objectivity, the mediator is not an authority on the truth in this matter, nor does the mediator hold the magic solution. Any particular analysis of the problem and the suggestions offered are filtered through the mediator's personal experiences and beliefs, and do not necessarily reflect what is best for the parties.

Rephrasing and Reframing

Rephrasing and reframing are techniques that can be used by a mediator to promote discourse, demonstrate empathy, and challenge the participants in a nonintrusive manner. There are many other techniques or interventions that can be identified to help with interpersonal communication. Therapists use techniques or strategies based on particular theories they adopt, as do lawyers, teachers, or any other practitioners whose trade involves relationships among people. Mediators can also pull from these other disciplines to find additional techniques or theories that might be helpful.

Rephrasing and reframing are techniques that may be universally helpful for any problem-solving facilitator. Every mediator should have these basic skills in his or her repertoire. Along with asking questions, rephrasing and reframing are among the most fundamental interventions for a mediator. Although practitioners may use different names to identify these particular techniques, rephrasing and reframing are performed by every mediator. One reason these techniques are so widely employed is because they are an inherent part of communication. These strategies are used naturally in everyday conversation, particularly when attempting to understand and acknowledge the feelings, ideas, or positions of another.

The mediator distinguishes between informal use of these techniques in everyday conversation and the employment of these strategies in a planned and deliberate manner. During mediation, the mediator often anticipates the responses that will be elicited by using these techniques. Rather than using only instinct and common sense to govern the flow of communication, the mediator plans when and how to intervene using rephrasing and reframing. The direction and success of the communication are governed less by instinct and more by design.

REPHRASING

Rephrasing involves rewording a statement made by someone else. The new words are different, but they convey the same meaning and spirit of the original statement. Rephrasing may be used to communicate information to others who are not present—for instance, to deliver information to an absent party during caucusing. Rephrasing is also used to communicate to the speaker of the statement that their message is clear, that there is no misunderstanding between the speaker and the listener. Rephrasing demonstrates a comprehension of the facts and a sensitivity for the spirit and intent of the message. Accurate rephrasing is often interpreted as empathy, which helps to build rapport.

Demonstrating Understanding

Rephrasing is a simple concept. The mediator merely restates the comments of the other person, but without repeating the same words. It is important to use different words that convey the same information and spirit because using new words indicates that the information has been internalized. Merely repeating someone's words does not convey an understanding of the message. Rephrasing using new language demonstrates that the ideas have been considered and comprehended. Rephrasing requires much more thought and consideration than merely repeating. The new statement can be evaluated for accuracy of content and intent.

In rephrasing, the person who made the original statement has the opportunity to judge whether the mediator has truly understood their meaning. This is important for both the participant and the mediator. Not only does this mollify the participant, but the mediator is assured that the interpretation is correct. This is critical for building trust, and also because a mediator is responsible for transferring information between parties during private caucuses. The mediator must take great care to present information that is both accurate in content and spirit. By rephrasing, the mediator is much less likely to impose his or her own perceptions.

Hearing a rephrased statement is comforting to a participant who is worried that the mediator may convey information inaccurately during a caucus. Although the parties understand that some information will be revealed in their absence, they may wish to maintain control over the details and the tenor of the conversation. In many cases, one of the initial causes of the conflict was miscommunication. The parties may therefore be concerned that further misinformation will complicate the problem. Of course, this a concern for the mediator as well. Sharing information during caucusing should never exacerbate the problem. Rephrasing is valuable for promoting confidence in the caucusing process; both the participant and mediator are assured that further miscommunication will not occur from relaying misinformation.

Protecting the Process

Rephrasing also acts as protection in the unlikely event that a party challenges the work of the mediator after the fact. It is possible that a person who is dissatisfied or disillusioned with the mediation process will blame the mediator for what is perceived as a failure of the process. There are many reasons someone might feel uneasy after the conclusion of mediation. In most instances, the discontent is not a reflection of the mediator's work. Not all cases are resolved to the complete satisfaction of the parties. A person placing blame for a disappointing resolution may be grasping for an explanation as to why mediation did not produce more favorable results.

Whatever the motivation of a discontented party, the mediator must contend with any accusation of substandard work. Once the mediation session is over there is little the mediator can do to comfort a distressed person. The mediator must look for signs of discomfort during the process and employ strategies to prevent or assuage any disquiet. Using the rephrasing technique is an effective way to assure the participants that their positions and wishes are respected. An accurately rephrased statement is concrete evidence that the mediator is alert, conscientious, empathetic, and competent. Participants who feel assured by techniques such as rephrasing are much less likely to point a finger if the outcome of the mediation does not meet expectations.

Modeling Productive Behavior

Rephrasing is also a chance to model good listening and understanding skills. Throughout the mediation process the mediator is modeling behavior that the parties can emulate. The mediator is considered by the parties to be an expert on problem solving. They will examine and reflect on what they learn from the mediator during the mediation process, which will be helpful both to resolve present and future disputes. Rephrasing is a simple technique that anyone can employ to assure clear understanding. Rephrased statements express concern, respect, and empathy, all very important features of productive and peaceful communication.

REFRAMING

While rephrasing aims to portray the exact meaning and intent of a statement, reframing involves a restructuring of ideas in order to identify an alternative connotation—in most instances, to present a more productive interpretation. Reframing entails translating or redefining a statement. In reframing, the general idea of the message is communicated, but the language is changed in such a way that the spirit or feeling is altered. Reframing is often used to make a comment appear more tactful and less critical or offensive. Reframing makes a statement more palatable to the receiver. It is also a tool to help the sender of the message discover a new conception of the idea. It helps the sender to reevaluate the intent of the message and its potential consequences.

Reconceiving Issues

It is true that reframing is an attempt to alter the sentiment or mood of a statement; this may require amending the content. Consider the earlier proposal, that truth is simply the story adopted as true. Reframing is very different from rephrasing, where remaining true to the content and feeling of the statement is the goal. In rephrasing, the mediator aims to assure the partici-pant that the message is clearly understood. This is an essential part of build-ing trust and accurately understanding the problem. But simply being able to reiterate what a person intends, generally, does not help to transform the problem in order to reach mutual resolution. To get to this important phase, reconceiving the issues, some intervention must be employed that leads a per-son to this new understanding.

The mediator can take a more passive stance, assuming that through the ac-tive communication encouraged by mediation, the parties will reevaluate the situation entirely on their own. Some mediators believe that ensuring total autonomy is the most appropriate way to handle mediation; it avoids any risk of imposing unwanted ideas onto the process. But many mediators, coun-selors, or other helping practitioners, are certain that in most cases a facilitator must take affirmative steps to guide people toward a novel way of thinking. This is the purpose of reframing—to offer alternative possibilities.

Reframing is not designed to insist, impose, or plant ideas into the minds of the parties, and it is certainly not intended to manipulate people into ac-tion. Even if this tactic were proper, which it is not, it would be useless in the long run. People who are coerced into taking action will not adhere to an agreement. Any hesitation, resentment, confusion, or discomfort felt after the mediation session is over will likely cause the destruction of the agreement and ultimately greater conflict.

Presenting Possibilities. Reframing can be conceived of as the presenting of possibilities. As a third party new to the dilemma, the mediator is in a unique position to view the problem objectively. An unbiased mediator, in-tently focused on the specifics of the problem, has the capacity to recognize dynamics that the parties are too entrenched in to identify. The mediator should present options that are novel and insightful, options not limited by business agendas, personal needs, and emotions. This is a tremendous asset to the parties, who sincerely wish to resolve the problem but have encountered barriers making resolution impossible. By reframing, suggesting subtle changes to the perspective presented, the mediator helps the parties consider new ways to view the problem, their opponent, themselves, and possible so-lutions. Reframing is the telling of a new story.

De-emphasizing Emotion. Reframing often de-emphasizes the emotional. For instance, if the message conveys intense anger that would likely trigger a series of hostile retorts, the message can be reframed less aggressively. For ex-ample, a participant might say: "I am sick and tired of that bastard lying to me. First Joe ignores everything I say, then he steals the important work from behind my back without a word. I just can't trust that creep." A reframing of this statement might be: "You are clearly very frustrated with the situation. You feel there is a lack of communication and you are left out of the loop. You want the opportunity to choose more of your work assignments and you would like more information about what goes on day-to-day in the office."

On paper, reframing may sound false; it may not convey the intensity of the emotions expressed. But reframing is not fake or patronizing—it is a genuine attempt by the mediator to reconstruct an idea in a more functional way. When reframing is performed in a live session, the mediator puts a great deal of effort into understanding the original statement. The statement is then tailored to be acceptable as a more productive way of viewing the problem. The participant has absolute and final authority to accept or reject a reframed statement. If the reframed statement does not accurately portray the content, the participant is encouraged to clarify and alter the reframe.

Reframing is good for handling volatile comments. When dealing with statements that are inflammatory, but also expressions of true feelings, rephrasing the comment demonstrates empathy and helps to build rapport. "I understand how angry you feel. You have tried to talk with Joe many times and you feel like you can never get a straight answer. I can imagine how infuriating that must be for you." The mediator never agrees with the perception but does acknowledge the feelings. Now, the mediator explains the reason for toning down the sentiment. "The problem I see is that, if I use your exact words, I suspect Joe will feel I am personally attacking him. That is not my role and I don't think it would be productive. I am here to help resolve a fight, not feed the fire." The mediator has now requested permission to present the reframed idea to the opposing side and indirectly pointed out a destructive and fruitless pattern of arguing.

As an intrinsic part of the mediation process the mediator has been afforded the right to translate information. As long as basic facts are not altered, the mediator does not need explicit permission to reframe a message for the other side. The mediator has made a clear promise to act impartially. When moving from one private caucus to another, the participants certainly do not expect that the mediator will intentionally infuriate the other side. The mediator is therefore free to reframe any message without previewing it for the sender. At the heart of reframing is simple diplomacy. It is a way to remove some of the most raw emotion and instead focus on the underlying problem.

Amplifying Emotion. While reframing is most often used to soften emotional undertones, it can also be used to amplify the emotional character of a message. There are many ways of handling stressful or frustrating situations. Many people react to conflict with heightened emotional reactions, but some individuals may disassociate or deny any emotional response. Other people may not internalize conflict and perceive it less as a personal affront. Still others may honestly be detached from the problem, simply having no emotional response to an issue that seems removed from them. To a person deeply affected by a conflict, this lack of emotional connectedness by an opponent may be perceived as a lack of interest or concern. In this case, reframing can be used to focus more directly on whatever concern has been shown in order to help to satisfy or comfort someone who feels disregarded or disrespected.

In a situation in which a participant is upset because the other side "doesn't care" or "doesn't understand how it feels," it is appropriate to reframe information using heightened emotional language, as long as the meaning of the message is not altered. For example, assume in response to the reframed message above, the other side responds with: "I really don't understand what the problem is. I just do my job and keep my mouth shut. Helen thinks there is a hidden agenda in everything I do. It's crazy. To tell the truth, I didn't even realize there was a problem here. I'm oblivious to office politics."

In relaying this message it might be helpful to say: "I have spoken with Joe and it seems to me that he is a very private person. He says he is used to a work environment where people work very independently. He didn't realize that you found his habits upsetting. From our conversation it seems Joe would be happy to figure out a way to prevent any more disruption or confusion in the office." Everything in this statement is accurate, but it is simply couched in a more sensitive and emotional tone. Hearing this reframed statement will be the first step in breaking through the hostility Helen feels. As long as Joe continues to participate in negotiations, which he has agreed to do by attending mediation, it is likely that the perceptions and attitudes of both sides will change.

Maintaining Impartiality

While the mediator should use reframing during mediation, and feel confident about the efficacy of this technique, using reframing may lead to the misrepresentation of ideas. The mediator must remain impartial, not impose on the parties, and refrain from tactics that distort wants and needs. The mediator must permit self-determination. Reframing used too freely can breach these fundamental tenets of mediator ethics.

To prevent the misuse of reframing techniques the mediator should never employ reframing as a tactic to mislead or manipulate the parties. Reframing should be employed frankly and openly. The parties must know that the mediator is making adjustments to the ideas presented. They must understand that they are free to reject the mediator's new interpretation and should never feel intimidated to do so. Reframing is a collaborative effort; ideally the mediator and the participants should work together to design a reframed idea that is both accurate and productive. Some reframing is done out of the speakers' presence without their involvement. But throughout the session the mediator has been working with the participants to understand their positions and feelings so clearly that a trust is formed, allowing the mediator to reframe based on true understanding.

Reframing is a technique used to begin a dialogue about options. The parties will appreciate an objective perspective as long as it is presented with respect, empathy, and consideration for their strongly held positions. Reframing involves a partnership and an exploration of ideas. It is a tool for reconceptualizing relationships and the stories that define the parties and their problem.

Coping with Emotions

During mediation emotions may run high. There is an important emotional element to all conflict, even conflict that on the surface appears to concern only business issues. This dynamic is more obvious in a workplace where conducting business requires close quarters and constant communication. But conflict has an emotional element even when the parties are much farther removed.

Even situations that on the surface do not seem to have an emotional component often do. For instance, some cases involve two parties in a dispute and an insurance company. When mediating those cases it is often clear that the two parties have an emotional involvement with each other and there may be interpersonal dynamics at play—issues of power and control, personal responsibility, fairness, and a host of other concerns. What may be surprising is that even the people working for the insurance company may present an emotional response.

While an insurance agency is an emotionally unencumbered business entity focused on securing and disbursing money, the insurance agents are people. These people are influenced by their clients, their personal sense of justice, and the realities of their job. It is not uncommon for an insurance agent to make reference to the way a party has treated the claim, the company, or the agent, personalizing what seems to be a sterile business transaction.

TYPES OF RESPONSES

It is difficult to gauge what form an emotional response will take. People vary in their responses to hurt feelings, fear, embarrassment, and anxiety. Some people cry, others become argumentative or verbally confrontational, still others become meek and avoid communication. In many cases an emotional response will be apparent, as with tears or raised voices. At other times, people will be adept at hiding their emotional responses. It is not the place of the mediator to attempt to draw out emotion—mediation is not therapy. But the mediator should allow people to express themselves as needed, and demonstrate empathy, encouraging the other party to demonstrate empathy as well.

Handling Emotion

Some people have difficulty handling the emotional responses of other people. Displays of emotions sometimes make people uncomfortable and insecure. In mediation there is the added difficulty that the people involved often have some personal responsibility for each others' feelings. The mediator is usually a stranger, not familiar with the participant's typical behaviors. It is normal for people to become ill at ease when they are confronted with the open expression of emotions. Emotions can be threatening on many levels and coping often feels like a test. To deal with most emotions, the same techniques described earlier can be employed: listening, showing empathy, asking questions, rephrasing, and reframing.

In most cases mediation will serve several important purposes with regard to emotions. First, there is a release of tension. The problems that lead to mediation can feel overwhelming and the experience of mediation may be a significant culminating event. Mediation is both the emotional height of the conflict and also the first opportunity to move away from the trouble. This release is often necessary and productive. Second, emotional responses often reveal that important information has been hidden. During an emotional breakthrough people feel justified in revealing issues they have previously held back. In part, the hidden issues cause the emotional response, and the emotional response permits the sharing of information. Emotion can indicate the significance of a concern when mere explanation cannot.

Most emotional responses evoked during mediation will be subdued, a raised voice, a moment of tears. The mediator should permit the expression of these feelings, even if this makes the session temporarily uncomfortable. The mediator and the parties can learn a great deal from a person who is freely expressing how he or she feels. It is also not the mediator's role to thwart or control people's responses. Mediation is designed to provide an opportunity for free expression; emotion is part of that process.

There are instances, however, when emotional outbursts become counterproductive. The mediator should not permit the participants to use emotion to manipulate or otherwise hinder the process. A screaming match will only serve to infuriate and reduce mutual understanding. Slinging insults is fruitless and damaging. The mediator makes a judgment call to draw the line and actively intervene. Some mediators use guidelines set at the beginning of the session as a reference, reminding participants of their promise to maintain mutual respect. The mediator can also redirect the participants by asking a question or making a suggestion. Often simply breaking the flow of the argument is enough to halt an escalation. The mediator must lead when the process is at risk, particularly if any participant's emotional or physical security is jeopardized. In extreme circumstances, the mediator can discontinue the session.

ANGER

It is almost inevitable that people will lose patience during mediation. People may also demonstrate hostility or belligerent attitudes. These may be directed toward the other party or toward the mediator. It is reasonable and expected that people will express strong negative emotions during mediation, particularly at the beginning of the process. Mediation by definition deals with volatile issues that make people feel angry, frustrated, and hurt. These emotions can take many forms. Displays of negative emotion in the form of general hostility, snide remarks, interruptions, raised voices, insults, and tears are expected.

Complex emotions will often manifest as anger. This may be the safest way to express other emotions such as hurt, surprise, confusion, distrust, and fear. Anger is a veil for other emotions, only when the veil is lifted are the true emotions exposed. Anger is a protective response. Anger also halts the process. When a person is venting using an angry response, it is almost impossible to address the underlying issues that compose the conflict. It is therefore the mediator's job to assist the person to move past the anger so that the mediation can continue.

Dealing with Anger

The protocols for dealing with anger fall on a continuum, but the goal is to gain control. The party must gain control of his or her emotions and the mediator must gain control of the process. An angry person who is venting emotions in an aggressive manner has control of the interaction; at that moment, the wishes and intentions of other people are suppressed.

Anger and other aggressive emotions are reasonable responses to conflict and the parties are entitled to express themselves. Empathy and sensitivity toward the angry party are appropriate when the person is merely venting frustrations. However, if these emotional expressions become destructive to the process, or damaging to an individual, it is the mediator's responsibility to regain control by halting the behavior. The most productive way to do this is to redirect the angry person.

Redirection involves helping the person to express emotion differently, calming the aggressive impulse. Assertiveness may be used when an angry person is out of control or using aggression to manipulate, but the mediator should never challenge or belittle an angry person. The mediator does not want to humiliate or feed a power struggle. Angry people can and will win a battle when challenged because they have the power to destroy the process.

Redirecting. In redirecting it is useful to first acknowledge the validity of the emotion. Use a statement such as: "I can see you are very angry right now. I appreciate how angry this situation makes you." Expressions of empathy help to build trust and can cushion an attempt to redirect the person to behave more appropriately. Further state: "I can tell you feel very strongly, but I am a little confused right now. I will understand the situation much better if you express yourself more calmly; why don't you start from the beginning and help me understand?" Asking for a favor or suggesting that a change in attitude will help the mediator is a way to redirect without accusing the person of immature or offensive behavior. Also, asking a person to back up and restate the story rationally may encourage them to review the situation in a new light.

Use of Authority. Although it is rare, a person truly out of control will require the mediator to be authoritative. If violent or extreme displays of anger occur, the mediator must take charge. At a minimum the mediator should suggest a private caucus. The mediator does not want to dismantle mediation prematurely. Anger can be mere performing, using aggression as an attempt to manipulate. In this case, removing the audience to whom it is directed may quell the outburst.

If a person becomes completely uncontrollable, the mediator should terminate the mediation. The mere suggestion of termination may be sufficient, but if there is any threat of violence, end the mediation quickly and calmly. The mediator should be firm when necessary, but never abuse power. Ideally, any intervention will dispel the outburst but keep the mediation going. Most of the time, momentary hostility is quickly forgotten.

Confidentiality

When designing a mediation program for any workplace, the most commonly raised issues relate to confidentiality. A workplace is like a small town, but with less privacy and personal space. Information travels fast and easily becomes distorted. Many employees claim that the grapevine is one of the biggest threats to the work environment. Although in most cases the passing of information is not intended to cause harm, this very normal human inclination can be very destructive. Whether or not the problems that arise from grapevine gossip are genuine threats to job stability or only perceived threats, fear of gossip is a hazard for any mediation program.

In all mediation programs, as in most other helping programs, confidentiality protections are included to guard participants from genuine and imagined risks. One reason that helping practitioners promise confidentiality is to calm the fears of the participants who worry that their private business will become public knowledge. This type of confidentiality agreement is between the participant and the practitioner. The practitioner promises not to discuss private information outside the helping session. Practitioners who violate this promise risk destroying the trust of clients, which at a minimum harms clients and ruins professional practices, and in some cases subjects the practitioners to professional or legal sanctions. Professional mediators who perform services for a fee may be subject to penalties for a breach of confidentiality.

The other form of confidentiality agreement that is in place for some types of helping professionals goes beyond the practitioner and the client and involves an additional promise assured by law. This type of confidentiality is called a "legal privilege." Lawyers, and sometimes doctors, therapists, and clergy, are granted a legal privilege. The purpose of legal privilege is to assure that people get the help they need without fearing that the government will step in and request private information. Legal privilege is based on a different rationale than described above. It is not to protect clients from hurtful or embarrassing gossip, but rather to encourage clients to be forthright in sharing perhaps self-incriminating information so that practitioners are able to give adequate treatment or representation.

Although there is no professionally or legally sanctioned requirement for confidentiality in peer workplace mediation, there remains a strong need for this protection. For the same reasons stated above, confidentiality in workplace mediation is essential. And, like professional organizations or the legal system, employers can and should set procedures for confidentiality and consequences for its breach.

Confidentiality is a simple concept, yet pragmatically difficult to maintain. In general, confidentiality is the promise that all the information shared during mediation will remain private. In mediation, confidentiality takes several forms. First, there is the assurance that the mediator gives to the parties. In the work setting, this confidentiality promise mandates that the mediator not share any information learned during mediation with the employer or other employees. There is also a promise made by the mediator that no information furnished during caucusing will be shared with the other side without explicit permission. Both of these promises, while absolutely essential to the process, can cause a number of problems.

Participants bring quite personal and volatile issues to the mediation. The process of mediation requires a trust that promotes sharing these private matters. In the work setting many of these private matters involve other people in the workplace. Information will often include negative sentiments about these people, feelings of anger, distrust, fear, accusations of incompetence and betrayal—all of which can potentially do a great deal of harm if exposed. There may also be information regarding private business matters. Revelations about these matters could result in interpersonal conflict and may hinder business functioning. From both personal and business perspectives it is essential that the mediator honor confidentiality promises or risk causing great harm.

Any concern that confidentiality will not be maintained results in serious hindrances for a mediation program. People will not participate fully if they are suspicious about how information will be used in the future. One of the most common reasons people refrain from volunteering for mediation, or are guarded during the process, is a sense of distrust. This distrust may be directed toward the mediator personally, but more often stems from a general sense of distrust that comes from past experiences in the workplace. People are painfully aware of how swiftly information travels on the job and also how it then becomes distorted. Virtually everyone who has ever been employed has had a least one personally or professionally devastating experience precipitated by gossip.

REVEALING INFORMATION

While the mediator must promise confidentiality, there will be times when the mediator wishes to share information outside mediation. Every mediator must contend with the natural human urge to discuss their experiences or, in other words, gossip. Most often gossip is not intended to cause harm and emerges from an interest in people and their circumstances. Discussing ourselves and others helps us understand and cope with life. Perhaps the entire world can be viewed as one large grapevine; people learn about each other through sharing interesting information. However, despite the understandable desire to discuss private matters for personal interest, a mediator simply must refrain from speaking about mediation. A mediator who cannot do this will inevitably cause suffering.

For Professional Growth

An ethical dilemma arises when a mediator believes outside discussion is necessary for professional learning and growth. Sharing "war stories" or seeking advice are important parts of developing one's skills. A mediator will often wish to address concerns with friends and colleagues in order to examine practice techniques and critique practice theories. A mediator may also be tempted to reveal mediation stories to relieve personal stress. Discussing work with respected people is important, and for a mediator this may involve revealing private information.

It is unrealistic to suggest that a mediator should never discuss cases outside of mediation. It would be destructive to mediation practice to forbid discussion undertaken for the purpose of learning. Most helping practitioners address this dilemma by making distinctions about how information will be shared. Practitioners often discuss their cases for the purpose of professional growth, with identifying information expurgated. Names and details are changed so that no link can be made between the story and particular people or organizations.

In a workplace setting where people know each other well, it may be very difficult to obscure the identities of the participants. Therefore, it is incumbent on in-house workplace mediators to avoid referring to actual cases with colleagues. Workplace mediators must use extreme care in protecting the confidentiality of the parties.

Requests from Employers

There are additional complications with confidentiality in a workplace setting. Because of the nature of the issues addressed, an employer may want to be informed about mediation discussions. Employers have various motivations for pursuing this information. Employers desiring greater control over the workforce may wish to use mediation information as a tool to consolidate their power. Employers may also wish to use information in order to monitor behavior and production. Many of the secrets revealed during mediation can be useful to an employer seeking to eliminate disruptive, unproductive, or unwanted workers. Information might also help to improve working conditions, to thwart inappropriate behavior, or to head off more severe conflict. The latter rationale for seeking information is reasonable and the workforce might actually benefit from the resulting positive change.

While it may be rational for the employer to seek information learned during mediation, this practice is inherently dishonorable. Mediation must remain private and confidential or there is a risk of destroying the program and infuriating the workers. Confidentiality pledges of a mediation program must guard against these interferences. A mediation program designed with ulterior motives is a guaranteed failure.

Any scheme created by an employer to misuse mediation will be exposed quickly and employees will refuse to fully participate. Although it is possible to require attendance at mediation, it is impossible to force open communication. Mediation under these conditions is pointless and more detrimental to an organization than offering no program at all. A covert program is based on lies and manipulation; an employer would fare better in the long run settling for inaction.

LEGAL EXCEPTIONS

While mediation information must remain confidential in most instances, there are a few circumstances when a mediator may be required to breach confidentiality. These include information related to behavior prohibited by law, such as discriminatory or criminal activity; information required by court order; and information necessary to defend against a complaint filed against the mediator. A workplace mediation policy may also include limited confidentiality exceptions for behavior prohibited by formal organization policy, such as dangerous or socially inappropriate activity or sexual misconduct.

WORKPLACE POLICY

A workplace mediation program must have clearly established policies regarding confidentiality breaches. Individual mediators should not be responsible for determining what kind of information may or may not be shared with an employer. Only in very rare instances should a mediator be required to reveal information at all.

To protect the parties, the mediator, the employer, and the program, all policy concerning confidentiality should be well documented and accessible to everyone in the workplace. Comprehensive and specific guidelines for sanctions should also be established in program policy. It is best to preempt all controversy by detailing protocol in writing. With regard to procedure, a mediation program should be designed to avoid on-the-spot judgment calls that might result in unequal treatment.

For a workplace mediation program to be successful, the employer must assure that mediation remain private and confidential. An employer should request information only when it is absolutely necessary for organizational administration or legal protection. The mediation process cannot be a ruse for instigating disciplinary action. Besides being unethical, it will not work. People will not participate in mediation if they do not believe it is safe and fair.

EXCEPTIONS TO CONFIDENTIALITY

Because of the importance of developing trust in the mediator and the mediation process, mediators commonly insist on confidentiality with a zeal that may be misleading, promising absolute confidentiality without qualification.

A participant's main concern is that their problems will not become fodder for office gossip. They are also concerned that the information they share will not be used against them later. For these reasons, a mediator must pledge confidentiality. However, mediators must acknowledge that there are exceptions to maintaining confidentiality and a promise to keep secrets may not be absolute.

Complying with Agreements

Circumstances can occur in the workplace that may compel the parties to share information in order to comply with agreements. The employer, supervisors, or other coworkers may need to know some details about an agreement in order to adhere to that agreement. The policies of the mediation plan should set forth the basic procedures for sharing information.

For instance, policy might direct immediate supervisors to oversee agreements and aid in their implementation. This policy is intended to make implementing agreements possible in a setting in which outsiders are often involved in completing tasks. The employer should never require revealing more information than necessary to assure compliance with agreements. Policy should limit information sharing unless absolutely necessary, and set sanctions.

Party Confidentiality Agreements. In addition to the requirements set by the employer, the participants should design individual agreements that expressly address confidentiality. These "party confidentiality agreements" should be created in the regular course of mediation. The party confidentiality agreement is a signed contract between the parties affirming that all mediation conversation will remain confidential. The parties may also agree to make exceptions to this rule and explicitly designate which information will be shared, with whom, and under what circumstances.

Party confidentiality agreements should be composed at the end of the mediation session in conjunction with a "memorandum of agreement" detailing the outcome of the mediation. As with all other volatile aspects of the mediation program, sanctions for breach of this agreement should be included in the program procedures.

The Legal Process

The most serious threat to confidentiality exists when a dispute escalates into a formal legal proceeding. Conflicts on the job do turn into legal battles on a fairly regular basis. Mediation cannot resolve every dispute and mediation does not prevent the filing of lawsuits. If an issue cannot be settled in-house, there is always the potential that the dispute will become more serious and involve the courts. Preventing court involvement is an important incentive for an employer to implement a workplace mediation program. But when the mediation program fails to resolve the problem, the courts may be enlisted.

If a legal case results from a previously mediated workplace conflict, there is some risk that the mediator will be called to testify as a witness. While this scenario is unlikely, it is not inconceivable. Mediators are not immune from being called as witnesses in court. They do not have a legal privilege, as do lawyers or doctors. Professional mediators generally address this issue by including a written clause in the agreement to mediate signed by both parties. This clause states that the parties agree that the mediator will not be called to testify in a legal proceeding. It also specifies the exceptions to the confidentiality agreement. This written notice serves as a legally binding contract that most courts will honor. Peer mediators should obtain a similar written agreement using a standard form designed for the workplace mediation program.

In reality, the likelihood that a peer mediator in a workplace program will be called into court is slim. Nonetheless, any person may be called into court as a witness at any time. There is perhaps no greater probability that a mediator will be called as a witness than any other coworker. People who have pertinent information are imposed on by our legal system and it is impossible to predict when such a situation will occur. The potential threat of having to testify in court should not discourage people from becoming mediators, although precautions should be taken with a written agreement. A written agreement not only protects the parties and the mediator, but also gives notice to the parties. If the written contract assuring nondisclosure is not accepted by the court, or a confidentiality exception applies, the parties have been warned. People engaging in a legal action should understand that information will be drawn from all possible sources.

Legal concerns are not raised as an attempt to spark fears or doubt in the process. However, the mediator and the parties should be aware of the potential paths unresolved conflict can take. All individuals who act as mediators, in any setting, should consider the issues surrounding confidentiality and the significance of that promise. But when considering these issues, keep in mind that mediation is an excellent way to address disputes so that they never rise to the level of legal action. A workplace mediator can help the parties resolve their problem peacefully and privately, therefore preventing more stressful and prolonged entanglements.

Confidentiality During Caucusing

Maintaining confidentiality during the caucusing process presents additional concerns for the mediator and the parties. Of course, all the promises made regarding confidentiality apply to both group sessions and caucusing. The confidentiality of shared information after the mediation process remains the same. There is no difference between group information and caucusing information in terms of confidentiality in relation to nonparticipants.

Information that is shared in private during a caucus must be regarded as confidential. Caucusing can be the most revealing stage of the mediation. The parties are usually eager to reveal the hidden or controversial aspects of the problem. As secrets are revealed, the issue of confidentiality can become tricky for the mediator. On the one hand, the mediator has made a promise to keep information confidential. On the other hand, if there is no flow of information back and forth it is difficult to move forward with the process. The mediation process itself is about sharing information, communicating. During caucusing the mediator becomes an intermediary and a filter for information. Information must move between the parties; caucusing is merely an alternative means of conveyance.

As the mediator travels between the parties, engaging in detailed discussion of the problem, the mediator must decide when and how to reveal the pertinent information without revealing secrets. The concept that all information will remain confidential does not apply during the caucus since one of the functions of caucusing is to aid in sharing information that was otherwise difficult to tactfully reveal. As a trained intermediary the mediator has the skills and objectivity to express the valuable information in an appropriate manner while still protecting privacy.

Perhaps the most important skill the mediator must master is sifting information. It is here where rephrasing and reframing become essential. The job the mediator performs during caucusing is the definitive mediator responsibility. Much of the assessment and decision making occurs on the spot, requiring continuous discernment. Mistakes made by the mediator can potentially destroy the process and harm the participants. While there are no hard-and-fast rules regarding handling specific information, since all information changes with each mediation, there are general principles that mediators follow during caucusing.

The first step is to reach an agreement with the parties about how information will be shared in general. Two broad alternative perspectives identify how sharing occurs while maintaining confidentiality. These of course are theoretical categories and do not precisely mirror actual practice. Some mediators choose to share all information with the other side unless explicitly instructed to withhold particular details. Other mediators take an opposite approach and share no information unless explicit instructions are given to share those particular details. The two approaches emerge from stylistic and philosophical differences. Most mediators plan to follow one approach and present only that option to the parties.

Arguably both approaches end in the same result: the mediator shares the information that is authorized and doesn't share information that is deemed private. No mediator would intentionally share information against the wishes of a participant. The difference in these approaches reflects the level of caution the mediator wishes to impose on the process. Neither approach is inherently better and both present valuable protections and difficult hurdles. For instance, mediators whose policy is to reveal nothing without permission must remember to obtain approval before every shift in conversation. Mediators who reveal everything except what is explicitly withheld require the parties to monitor themselves and the mediator carefully, which may hinder the openness of communication.

THE ALTERNATIVE PROCESSES

Although the two processes are conceptually different, in practice they may appear quite similar. The mediator must remain flexible and reflect the needs and wishes of the parties, even if adaptation produces contradiction. However, in order to break the rules, rules must first be imposed. Examining each perspective more closely will help the mediator to gain a clearer understanding of what may occur and predict probable scenarios. A mediator should understand the purpose and ramifications of each alternative, choose one to apply, yet be willing to alter the plan when needed.

Sharing Everything

In the first alternative the mediator proposes sharing all information with the other side unless explicitly instructed to withhold particular details. Of course in practice the mediator does not literally do this. A mediator will only share useful information that could be productive to the process. Information is also rephrased and reframed to make it more tolerable.

This policy affords the mediator the freedom of a naturally flowing conversation. Using this approach, the mediator has more decision-making authority and is freer to make spontaneous decisions without first initiating a conference. This policy gives the mediator a great deal of control and may encourage the mediator to make determinations that go beyond the scope of the mediator role. Without explicit permission, the mediator may share information that the party preferred to keep secret, but for some reason did not identify. Since each party is not present at the other caucus, and cannot read the mediator's mind, it is very difficult for the parties to predict what the mediator will and will not share.

Sharing Nothing

The alternative policy—share no information unless explicit instructions are given to share those particular details—serves to protect the parties more fully. There is less risk that the mediator will reveal secrets and upset the parties. But it also can make conversation more cumbersome. The mediator is forced to rehearse everything before meeting with the next group. This can disrupt the normal flow of thought and can be time-consuming. The parties may actually become annoyed with this convoluted process that can make conversation seem fake and unnatural. Of course, if a party neglects to clearly identify a secret, there is no worry that it will be shared accidentally, and this may be very comforting to participants.

Combined Approach

In practice, most mediators probably lean toward a middle or combined approach. A mediator will share some information without the explicit permission of the parties, but is careful to gain permission before revealing anything that even suggests the need for privacy. Here, the mediator is responsible for making independent determinations about what might be private, but still errs on the side of caution. The mediator is sure to review or rehearse any information if there is the slightest chance for confusion or misinterpretation. However, information that is clearly not volatile will be shared naturally in the course of conversation. Employing this combined approach presents some risk of misinterpretation and unauthorized revelation. But if the mediator is thorough in asking questions and uses rephrasing and reframing techniques, there should be few mistakes.

Regardless of which approach the mediator chooses, the parties will usually identify sensitive information. Participants often preface comments with: "Of course this is confidential" or "This is between us." When a party explicitly identifies confidential information, it is wise to offer reassurance that privacy will be honored. Reassurance facilitates building trust.

At times a mediator may feel that some information held secretly would greatly benefit the process if shared. The mediator has the right and responsibility to mention this thought. Once expressed, the mediator must be careful not to pressure or manipulate the participants into revealing details they truly do not wish to share. A mediator should make observations and even suggestions, but always in the spirit of respectful and collaborative assistance.

Because the parties are not present at each other's caucusing sessions, they may become curious or even paranoid about what is discussed without them.

While each side is perfectly aware that they are being discussed, this reality can make anyone insecure, particularly when the discussion is about a private and difficult problem. To comfort the parties about these secret meetings, it is helpful to debrief each side during caucusing. Debriefing simply involves keeping the parties informed, and frequently detailing what was already shared and what is intended to be shared in the future. This may require repeating stories several times, but it is a valuable tool for easing fears.

When debriefing the parties about the last round of caucusing, the mediator must remember to adhere to the confidentiality plan. There will be substantial discussion between the mediator and each party that will never be discussed publicly. Despite the fact that each side is curious about what transpired in the other caucus, most of what is discussed remains confidential. Regardless of which approach is taken, the mediator only shares information valuable to the resolution process. Of course, resolution is greater than the final agreement; resolution encompasses building empathy, strengthening communication, and defusing anger and frustration.

It is the responsibility of the mediator to be cautious about how and when to share information. It is an abuse of power to intentionally initiate dialogue that will cause harm. In protecting confidences during caucusing, the most serious risk to the mediator and the parties lies in the momentary lapse. In the heat of the moment, and with sincere desire to help, a mediator may unintentionally reveal a confidence. This might occur accidentally when blurting out information without proper forethought, or more likely by wording a statement in such a way that information is implied.

Inexperienced mediators are particularly at risk for this type of mistake when posing questions that were sparked by a discussion with the other side. Mistakes may also occur when reframing information between parties. A mediator must always be self-aware. Even when the discussion is flowing naturally, which is ideal for building trust, the mediator must continue to measure his or her own words. Caucusing is like a dance. The parties choreograph the routine and the mediator is a dancer, moving gracefully between the parties, but always reflecting the choreographers' design.

Mediation Notes

During a mediation session most mediators choose to take notes. Written notes are useful for remembering details easily forgotten. It is important to keep track of details because asking for the same information may suggest to the parties that the mediator is not attending. Taking notes fosters the appearance that the issues being discussed are significant. This is both helpful for the mediator and lends credence to the process.

For many mediators, the majority of the note taking occurs during the opening remarks. This is the time when the mediator gains a broad idea of the problem. Technical matters will usually be mentioned at this time and it is a good opportunity for the mediator to identify issues and questions to address later on. The extent to which a mediator takes notes will depend on personal preference and the nuances of the case.

Although mediators should feel free to take notes as needed, it is important to balance writing with making eye contact. Writing furiously throughout the session does not leave much opportunity for personal connection with the participants. A mediator should not sacrifice building trust for compiling a complete set of notes. Once a true conversation begins, often during the caucusing phase, the mediator may want to focus more attention on the parties. At this point the mediator may jot down important points when they arise, but enough familiarity with the problem has been gained that natural back-and-forth conversation will be possible without constant reference to the notes.

The concerns surrounding note taking are generally identified by common sense. However, one important issue arises for all mediators that should be specifically addressed. Written notes taken during mediation create a record of events that can pose a possible confidentiality problem. These notes can be used by the mediator or by a third party to reveal information in the future, resulting in a serious breach of the confidentiality promise.

For instance, employers who are aware that mediation notes exist may be tempted to request them for review or, if accessible, review them covertly. It is difficult to control who will view paperwork stored at the workplace and there is always a possibility that mediation notes will get into the hands of the wrong person. Equally troublesome, if written notes exist, courts may be able to subpoena them more easily than demanding oral testimony. Memories fade, but written notes last forever.

Because of these risks, some mediators destroy their notes directly after the session. The safest way to prevent intentional or accidental exposure is to eliminate the evidence. There is no official governing body that regulates whether mediators keep or destroy their notes. Even if professional ethical standards existed, they would not likely apply in a workplace peer mediation setting. However, there are legitimate reasons to keep written notes and the decision belongs to the individual mediator. Although the trend seems to be to destroy notes, this should not be done without an examination of the pros and cons.

PROS

The following are some reasons that support destroying mediation notes:

1. In the event that the mediation is not settled and a legal action ensues, documentation that exists may be requested by the parties, the employer, lawyers, or the courts. This is the primary reason practitioners advocate destroying notes; paperwork that does not exist cannot be misused.

2. It is possible that an employer or coworker will choose to intercept mediation notes and use them as a way to learn about the mediation session. Employers have various motives for this practice, which may be prompted by either honorable or underhanded aims. Whatever the purpose, this interception breaches the confidentiality and privacy promised to the parties.

To prevent an employer from reviewing mediation notes if they are kept, they should not be stored on the workplace premises. If a mediator is concerned that the employer might somehow obtain notes that are stored outside the office, it is best to destroy them. A conscientious employer might consider designing a written policy and procedure for keeping, storing, and destroying the notes. These rules should be presented to everyone affected by the workplace mediation program, including the mediators, all employees, and management.

CONS

The following are some reasons that support keeping mediation notes:

1. Written notes may benefit the mediator for future educational and professional growth. Ideas may be sparked by a mediation session that prompt discussion with colleagues. Since mediators learn a great deal from talking with each other, it may be very helpful to have a reference during these conversations. There may also be an instance when a mediator wishes to refer back to their notes at a later time, either to clarify an issue for the parties or to use as a reference for a future case. Notes are a helpful reminder, which do not fade like the human memory.

2. A number of professional mediation associations exist nationwide. Many mediators belong to one or several of these associations that promote professional connections, offer discounted tuition for conferences, publish newsletters, and provide other membership benefits. At least one of these national mediation associations requires a membership application including the submission of case notes for re-

view. These notes, with client names changed, are used to determine mediator competency when applying for advancement in the organization.

3. Perhaps the most crucial reason to retain mediation notes is to maintain a record for personal protection. Although it is extremely unlikely, a small number of professional mediators have been sued for malpractice. In the instance that legal action is brought against a mediator for inadequate performance, the only concrete evidence of competent work is the notes taken during mediation sessions. In a workplace setting, it is conceivable that a disenchanted participant might complain to the employer about the perceived incompetence of a mediator. Again, written notes are the only proof of what occurred during the mediation.

However, it is important to keep any fears of retribution in perspective. Of all professional mediations held to date, it is reported that only a handful of malpractice suits have been filed, and these lawsuits were brought against mediators who charge a fee for service. Peer mediation in the workplace is not a professional paid service; it is a volunteer effort that carries no express or implied warranties. It is doubtful that a peer mediator could be sued for malpractice. Peer workplace mediators are volunteers in a field where no licensing is required, even for paid professionals. There are no generally accepted and regulated standards for practice in professional mediation, much less volunteer peer mediation. Proof of malpractice is therefore virtually impossible.

Although malpractice claims may be unlikely, a peer mediator might fear complaints lodged with the employer. In the course of a mediation program there will likely be some participants who are dissatisfied with the process. It is difficult to predict how any given employer will react to a complaint made against a peer mediator. The mediation program design in this text assumes that all mediators are volunteers, that the parties select a mutually agreed on mediator from a panel of mediators, and that mediators will never breach a promise of confidentiality. There should be no sanctions for poor performance, only for breaching confidentiality. If a complaint is made about a particular mediator, the employer should consider providing additional training or, in the extreme, removing the mediator from the panel. Any additional sanctions should be clearly defined in the mediation rules and procedures.

In sum, the personal protection that written notes may afford the professional mediator might be sufficient justification for keeping them. In the workplace, however, this practice is probably unnecessary. Peer workplace mediators should not fear reprisal for poor performance. It is understood that peer workplace mediators are not highly trained professionals. Nonetheless, the choice to keep or destroy notes should still be considered seriously. If a workplace mediator does elect to retain written notes, it is probably wise to store them at home and not on the job site where they may be viewed by the employer or coworkers.

As a further note on maintaining records, some employers might consider using other recording devices during mediation—for instance, audiotape or videotape. These devices are becoming ever more popular in the workplace for both learning and protection. However, they should never be used during mediation without the express permission of the parties. The employer and mediator must be vigilant against coercing the parties into taping.

Taping can be useful for training purposes and some parties may agree to have a session taped for this purpose. If a recording is made, the employer and the mediator must be absolutely clear about how the tape will be used, and must ensure that the parties are not confused about the purpose of the tape. Tapes should be made with caution and used and stored meticulously. Tapes present a risk to confidentiality and may make the parties uncomfortable during the session, affecting their behavior and the outcome of mediation.

Legal Privilege

"Legal privilege" is a concept that relates to confidentiality. It refers to the legal right of protection against government interference in private matters. It is the confidentiality protection afforded to the clients of lawyer, doctors, and sometimes other professionals. It permits the relationship between these clients and professionals to remain private; virtually no information produced in the course of this professional relationship must be revealed in court. This protection is designed to assure open communication and the best possible service. It is thought that if clients fear the government might intervene and obtain private information, they might hold back pertinent details and disrupt the delivery of service.

While legal privilege is not an issue that will affect most workplace peer mediators, it is an important concept to understand because of the confidentiality promises made during mediation. People in helping roles can unintentionally mislead their clients when they make promises of confidentiality. A promise made between individuals does not necessarily protect them from certain government interference, like the requirement of testifying in court. All mediators should know the limits of their confidentiality promise so they can accurately inform the parties.

Any mediator may potentially be called into court as a witness. Mediators are privy to a great deal of information that might be useful to the parties if a work conflict later becomes a court case. Although anyone on the job with relevant information is a potential witness, besides mediation, there are few instances between coworkers when promises of confidentiality have been made. The issue of privilege arises when a mediator makes a promise of confidentiality and then a legal proceeding requires that mediator to breach confidentiality.

While legal privilege overrides the requirement for a witness to reveal confidential information in a legal setting, as a general rule, no mediator/client relationship carries this legal privilege. In most cases a mediator can be compelled to reveal information in a legal setting regardless of the promise made to the parties. There may be exceptions to this rule, and it is possible that a judge would honor a written confidentiality agreement made between the mediator and the parties. However, neither the mediator nor the parties should rely on such an exemption. Hence, it is important for the mediator not to mislead the parties to believe that confidentiality is absolute.

UNDERSTANDING LEGAL PRIVILEGE

Privilege is a legal construct that is aimed at protecting privacy. In order to foster open and honest communication, privilege is granted between clients and certain professionals. Each state has its own privilege rules, but this protection generally applies to lawyers, medical doctors, and clergy. Some states extend or limit this privilege. The state "code" contains the legislation that defines the boundaries.

The basic concept of privilege is that the client/professional relationship may remain confidential; the professional cannot be compelled to testify in court about case-related conversations. Also, all related notes or "work product" created by the professional, as a result of the relationship, cannot be subpoenaed and used as court evidence. This is only a very basic outline of the privilege concept; different states have unique rules and interpretations of these rules.

The reason for this explanation of privilege is to indicate how infrequently it applies. Although many professionals promise their clients confidential communications, the legal system may not recognize that promise in a court setting.

Confidentiality protection in the mediation setting also varies from profession to profession. For instance, the clients of mediators licensed as lawyers may be afforded different confidentiality protection than the clients of mediators licensed as social workers or psychologists. Even within a profession, confidentiality protection may differ depending on the setting of the mediation. For example, in West Virginia, privilege only attaches when mediator lawyers practice in "court annexed" mediation, mediation directed and approved by the state court.

In addition, it is important to realize licenced helping professionals, such as social workers or therapists, will be required to adhere to their professional code of ethics when acting as mediators. For example, mediation does not wave the "legally mandated requirement to report suspicion of child abuse or a suspicion of bodily harm or violence to another person," as required by the NASW *Standards of Practice for Social Work Mediators.*

Consequently, mediators should be cautious about misleading mediation participants. Mediators must inform the parties that there are exceptions to confidentiality. Confidentiality exceptions may apply to information related to behavior prohibited by law, such as discriminatory or criminal activity, information required by court order, and information necessary to defend against a formal complaint filed against the mediator.

Final Agreements

If the parties have reached a favorable resolution at the close of a mediation session, a final agreement is written. Although the success of mediation cannot be measured by a mutually satisfactory resolution, an agreement is certainly one main goal of the process. There are many benefits to participating in mediation even if no final agreement is possible. However, there is great satisfaction when the parties, with the mediator's assistance, conclude the session with a concrete plan for resolution.

WRITTEN AGREEMENTS

Final agreements usually take the form of a written "contract," a document that represents a "meeting of the minds." This simple contract is merely a recap of the agreement in writing and signed by the parties. The mediator acts as a secretary, writing down the words, but does not sign the agreement. With this contract the parties assert they understand the agreement and consent to the terms. Any document that affirms an agreement evidenced by signatures is a contract. It is not necessary for lawyers to be involved to form a contract. It is common practice to form legally binding contracts without the aid of lawyers or judges—for instance, renting a videotape often requires a contract as does borrowing a library book.

It has been found that the parties are more likely to adhere to agreements that have been drafted in writing. A written agreement is also an important reference for reminding the parties of their exact agreement later on, when memories fade or if there is any future disagreement. Written agreements should be detailed enough that the parties have all the information they need to comply strictly with the resolution. The mediator should assist the parties in clarifying any ambiguities that are overlooked, such as exactly when and how a task will be completed. Mediators are concerned that the agreement will hold up over time; in other words, it should be sufficiently clear, does not cause future conflict, and promotes compliance without further intervention.

In addition to promoting adherence, written agreements about interpersonal issues help people to clarify issues and illustrate behavior change. Written agreements help build trust. An agreement can be a reference if future conflicts arise around the similar issues, and these agreements assist people in keeping commitments in the long term. Written agreements act as a psychological safety net, helping people to feel satisfied and confident in the work they have done and the resolutions they have made.

ORAL AGREEMENTS

In some instances there is no need for a written contract. Disputes between people that are interpersonal in nature or don't involve performing specific actions may not call for a written agreement. There are instances when the circumstance or personalities of the participants make a written agreement unnecessary or uncomfortable. For some people a handshake represents a serious commitment and forcing a written agreement would be an awkward exercise, causing more harm then good. The choice of whether to draft an agreement belongs to the parties, although many participants would never consider the idea without the suggestion of the mediator.

The mediator and the parties should feel free to do what makes most sense under the particular circumstances. Mediators tend to favor written agreements, but the parties may not. It is acceptable for a mediator to suggest a written agreement and explain to the parties the likely benefits, but, as with all aspects of mediation, the parties are entitled to make the final decision. If the parties decide against a written agreement and an oral agreement is chosen, the mediator should still assist the parties in clarifying the issues so that the details of the resolution are comprehensive and clear.

FAIRNESS IN AGREEMENTS

The issue of fairness in agreements is controversial. Mediators expect that a successful agreement will be designed to be fair. It is often assumed that fairness is critical for long-term compliance. Some mediators see themselves as arbiters of fairness. They take the position that if an agreement is blatantly unfair, the mediator is responsible to help rectify the discrepancy. These mediators will halt a process rather than allow an injustice to occur. Other mediators feel strongly that the subjective judgment of the mediator is not to be imposed on the parties regardless of the apparent inequity of the agreement. These mediators will not interfere beyond asking the parties to fully consider their decision.

It is an accepted principle of mediation that the parties have the right to self-determination. They have autonomy in decision making. It is also understood that problems brought to mediation are laden with emotion, frustration, confusion, and a variety of elements that cloud judgment. Given these features and some pressure to resolve the dispute, parties may misjudge the equity of an agreement. An agreement that is considered unfair on later reflection is doomed to long-term failure and may spur further conflict.

Fairness is always a difficult judgment call. Mediation embraces the notion that fairness is not always objective and the needs of people differ greatly. For instance, while one person views collecting money as a fair resolution, another seeks a sincere apology. Mediation is based partly on the principle that the rigid boundaries that define fairness in our bureaucracies, such as the legal system, do not reflect the needs of all people. Mediation offers dynamic and individually designed solutions that satisfy the personal desires of the participants. It is for this reason that the objectivity of the mediator can sometimes be a hindrance to achieving fairness; the mediator is not emotionally involved and cannot correctly weigh the subjective wishes of others.

Mediation is not ruled by a collective standard of justice, precedents and laws, a collective consciousness, or a moral or ethical authority. In mediation there is no outside arbiter of justice; the people involved must use their own judgment to determine fairness for themselves. The freedom and flexibility mediation permits is also a burden, as people intimately involved in a conflict must define fairness. In this context the mediator, while not an authority, is an important source of objective reflection. The mediator helps the parties examine their decisions in the light of an outside perspective.

Mediation is a trade-off. The parties increase their autonomy and gain independence from potentially oppressive decision making. In return they must demonstrate candor, thoughtfulness, sensitivity, and concern for others. Frankly, this may be an unreasonable expectation of some people in some circumstances. There are times when people are so angry or hurt that they simply cannot make clear judgments. And some situations are so egregiously unfair that no compromise could possibly lead to justice. There are also instances in which ulterior motives are so powerful that the parties truly cannot be trusted to make fair agreements. These are troubling dilemmas for a mediator who is committed to both fairness and self-determination.

Although the mediator has agreed to take an impartial stance, the mediator still assumes responsibility for what transpires during the process. Despite the fact that the mediator is not a decision maker, the parties are greatly influenced by what the mediator offers. The mediator directs the process, influences the flow of discussion, and helps to focus agreements by asking questions, posing possibilities, and challenging assumptions. Regardless of philosophy, the mediator has influence over the decisions made by the parties, and that influence is shaped by the mediator's personal belief system and sense of fairness.

Thus, the question remains: Where does the mediator draw the line in questioning the parties' sense of fairness? Obviously there is no pat answer. The mediator must use individual judgment, but should consider some basic principles.

Good Faith Negotiations

Prior to participating in mediation the parties sign an agreement to mediate. This agreement sets out the terms for mediation, including the requirement to negotiate fairly and in good faith. With this agreement comes a presumed trust. Of course the mediator does not have the power to guarantee the earnestness of the parties, but all the participants must assume that once this agreement has been made the discussion that follows will be forthright.

Independent Decision Making

Although it may be simpler for an objective outsider to design a rational solution to a problem, that outsider does not have to abide by the decision. Nor can that outsider fully understand the unique dynamics of the dilemma. If resolutions that meet very personal requirements could be successfully designed by outsiders, there would be no need for mediation. The purpose of mediation is to move away from authoritarian decision making. The parties take greater personal responsibility for their actions and the resolution of their problems. Mediation is a learning experience, not merely a forum for dismissing conflict.

Active Mediator Participation

There are instances when balanced mediation is impossible—for example, if parties are unable to advocate for themselves due to fear, intoxication, mental incapacity, or other infirmity. It then falls on the mediator to protect the integrity of the process. This may require halting the session, though many mediators would agree that even people with afflictions have the right to make their own decisions in mediation. In accepting the reality that the mediator does impact the process, the mediator is not passive. If the parties could settle the dispute without assistance, there would be no need for mediation.

COMPLYING WITH REGULATIONS

During mediation, questions often arise as to whether resolutions comply with regulations concerning workplace policy or relevant law. The parties turn to the mediator for guidance on these matters. The mediator must be cautious not to overstep the boundaries of the mediator role. The mediator is not responsible for monitoring compliance with outside rules. The parties maintain sole responsibility for gaining information.

Workplace Policy

In workplace mediation, workplace policy, or the reality of the participants' job duties, may determine the appropriateness of particular agreements. In many instances there will be restrictions on behavior that thwart the wishes of the parties. Parties must avoid resolutions that violate workplace policy. Clarifying limitations or restrictions is an important part of implementing a workplace mediation program. Setting guidelines should be the responsibility of the employer.

A mediator should not be required to enforce or monitor workplace policy. It is acceptable for the mediator to question parties about workplace regulations just as the mediator would inquire about any other aspect of the agreement. However, the mediator should not present factual information because this practice may lend the appearance of advocacy for a party or for the employer. Additionally, the mediator risks overstepping and offering the parties incorrect information. This is not a risk the mediator should take.

An employer may wish to set up a procedure for reviewing agreements after they are made to assure compliance with workplace policy. Limitations of any review should be strict, avoiding any breach of confidentiality. An employer might consider allowing agreements to be exercised as written until a problem arises; at that point the employer can require that the agreement be modified. These policy considerations are the responsibility of the employer and must not be left to the mediator.

The Law

Under no circumstances should a mediator offer any information that could be construed as legal advice. In fact, even lawyer-mediators are prohibited from offering legal information or advice during mediation. If an issue of legality arises, the parties remain free, and are encouraged, to seek the assistance of an independent attorney. Contracts are not as a rule required to meet legal standards. There is a saying in the law that people are free to write "bad contracts." The illegality of a contract does not necessarily void the contract; the fate of a bad contract is determined by a judge in litigation. Whether or not a contract meets legal requirements is not the responsibility of the mediator. All concerns about legality should be brought to an outside attorney.

Section II

EXERCISES

The following sections include exercises, concepts for consideration, and pointers. Working through these problems will aid the mediator in building skills. The exercises in this section mimic real-life situations. The questions posed are often challenging, and there is generally more than one productive reaction. Competent mediators adapt distinctive styles and responses to similar situations.

In examining these issues, it is valuable to consider both productive and destructive strategies. Mediators aim to assist the parties, but equal attention must be paid to avoiding harm. Consider also that the ideal approach may not always be possible in live situations. The goal of the mediator is to design responses that are reasonable, practical, and effective.

Part One

Addressing Conflict

Changing Circumstances

Conflict changes depending on the circumstances, the nature of the debate, and our opponent. Considering our real-life experiences and how they might change depending on the circumstances can be illuminating. Use the following questions to reflect on actual conflict and how it might be affected by altering surrounding circumstances.

I.

Consider a real-life heated disagreement that you have experienced. Choose one in which you and an opponent took a strong stance on an issue, in which the people involved took sides. This disagreement may have been with a family member, friend, or coworker. It could have been on any subject: politics, religion, love, money, children, or job duties.

Consider your position. You will notice that you had to develop coherent arguments. At the heart of debate is the attempt to convince your opponent that you are "right." To do this you must attempt to express rational positions; these positions are often called arguments.

1. What were the issues you debated about?
2. Did you take a side?
3. Did your opponent take the opposite side?
4. What arguments did you make to support your position?
5. What arguments did your opponent make to support his or her position?

6. Did you sincerely believe the arguments you were making?

7. Did you ever play the "devil's advocate"?

8. In retrospect, do you agree with any points your opponent made?

9. If you had the same argument today, would you change your position?

10. How did the passing time affect your position on the subject?

Pointer: During a debate we often make arguments that are in direct response to our opponent. These arguments do not always reflect our true beliefs and feelings. Statements are sometimes made for the sake of argument. The attitude and position of our opponent can have a great effect on the way we present our case.

11. How did your opponent's position affect the arguments you made?

12. Describe any positions you took for the sake of argument, things you said in order to win.

Pointer: Emotion has great impact in a heated debate. When we get angry, we say things we might not otherwise say. Emotion also leads to other responses—for instance, frustration, feelings of intimidation, and embarrassment. Our emotional response to our opponent will affect the arguments we make.

13. Describe your emotional response to your opponent's arguments.

14. How did your emotional responses affect the arguments you made?

Pointer: During a debate, many outside influences can have an impact on our actions. The "atmosphere" of the encounter and the surroundings can affect our style of argument. For instance, body language, the presence of others, fear that others are listening, physical discomfort, and our individual mood may influence our position.

II.

Picture the debate you described. Imagine changes in the atmosphere and surroundings. How might your style of argument have changed with the altered encounter?

1. If family members were listening.

2. If you were on a crowded street.

3. If your boss was listening.

4. If your opponent began to cry.

5. If your opponent began to scream and swear.

Imagine how the debate might have changed if:

1. Your opponent started to agree with you.
2. One person had to leave the room for ten minutes.
3. The debate had to stop and was continued a week later.
4. You found out your opponent had been lying.
5. A third person joined the debate, on your side.
6. A third person joined the debate, on your opponent's side.
7. One person said something very funny and you both began to laugh.
8. Your opponent began to laugh, at you!

Pointer: *The relationship you have with a person can greatly affect a debate. There is probably more freedom to express your mind with a spouse than with a boss. On the other hand, it is more likely that a heated disagreement will emotionally hurt a loved one than a colleague. The nature of the relationship will impact the benefits and losses incurred in any debate.*

III.

A debate on the same topic with different people will be a unique experience. Picture the debate you described. Consider how your arguments and style of communication would change with different people:

1. Your significant other.
2. Your mother.
3. Your boss.
4. Your subordinate at work.
5. Your child.

Pointer: *Think about the concept of "winning." Being the winner has both rewards and consequences. When there is a winner, there is usually a loser. If we have an ongoing relationship with the person who lost, we may also be affected by their defeat. A win/lose situation can alienate those close to us and weaken personal ties.*

IV.

How might winning a debate affect your relationships? What are the rewards and consequences of winning?

1. With your significant other.
2. With your mother.
3. With your boss.
4. With your subordinate at work.
5. With your child.

Gaining Greater Perspective

Reflect on the following scenarios and questions to examine how different roles require different perspectives. For instance, supervisors and subordinates view situations differently. Each of us will experience conflict from diverse and competing positions that will alter our perspective.

I.

You are the supervisor in a small office. You oversee the work of six employees. You have a boss who works in another office but calls each day to check up on you. You feel that your boss is unfairly demanding at times and expects you to have constant control over the behavior of your employees. When one of your employees makes a mistake, your boss blames you for ineffective management.

One of your workers has made a terrible error that can potentially cost the company a good deal of money. Although you don't think it was intentional, you think the employee was very sloppy and irresponsible. This kind of sloppiness seems typical of this worker and you have hinted at this several times. You have never had a formal discussion about the poor work, hoping that as he learned more he would improve independently. Now you are very angry, you are sure your boss will blame the mistake on you, and this seems so unfair. You call the worker into your office.

1. Describe your instinctive response to this situation.
2. Explain the thinking behind this response. What is your rationale for reacting this way?
3. How would you expect your own boss to respond to this situation?
4. What might be a more productive or effective response in this situation?
5. How are you most likely to get the result you most desire?

Consider these responses. What might result from each reaction?

- Describe every detail of the mistake to the employee and demand an explanation.
- Suggest that the employee is not living up to his potential—perhaps he is unhappy.
- Scold the employee for his incompetence. You won't tolerate such sloppy work.
- Take all the blame yourself. As the boss you are responsible for everything.
- Fire him.
- Offer the employee more training.
- Explain the pressures you are under and hope he will work harder to help you.

Consider these rationales. Are they productive ways to view problem solving?

- Intimidating the worker promotes a better job. Fear is a great motivator.
- Investigating what actually transpired is a good way to learn from our mistakes.
- Mediocre employees are useless. It is best to get rid of them right away.
- It's best to fix the problem right away. More training is how problems get solved.
- Playing on the sympathies of employees can motivate them to work harder.
- It's best to avoid conflict. It is never productive.
- Reputation is everything; acting as a neutral supervisor is essential for appearances.

Pointer: *Thinking about how people you know would respond to a situation can help you objectively evaluate positive and negative ways to deal with a problem.*

II.

The identical scenario has occurred, only now you are the employee who made the mistake. You are very upset at your mistake and worried about getting fired; your spouse is out of work and there are few other jobs in the area. You work hard and do your best under the circumstances. You are angry because you don't think you were properly trained. You really believe the whole thing was your supervisor's responsibility. You have never complained about your training because you thought it would only cause trouble and you didn't want your abilities questioned. Other than some snide comments, your boss has never complained before, but now you expect the worst.

1. Describe your instinctive response to this situation.
2. Explain the thinking behind this response. What is your rationale for reacting this way?
3. How would you expect a coworker you know to respond to the situation above?
4. What might be a more productive or effective response in this situation?
5. How are you most likely to get the result you most desire?

Consider these responses. What would result from each reaction?

- Defend yourself forcefully, while denying you made any mistake.
- Defend yourself forcefully, explaining you did your best under the circumstances.
- Blame your poor training.
- Ask how other employees do the task and compare yourself to them.
- Take full responsibility; apologize profusely.
- Blame the supervisor.
- Ask for suggestions and make a plan for the future.

Consider these rationales. Are they productive ways to view problem solving?

- Attributing the mistake to the circumstances is a good way to avoid criticism.
- Offering a thorough explanation is a good way to justify questionable actions.
- Laying the blame elsewhere keeps the focus on other people's abilities.
- Taking enough time to be fully informed will help in accomplishing the task properly.
- Avoiding conflict will smooth things over and prevent angry interactions.
- Playing on the sympathies of the boss is a good way to avoid punishment.
- Taking all the responsibility gets others off the hook, which helps build relationships.

Impartiality

Mediators must remain impartial even when they have strong personal feelings about the situation. Evaluate the proposed ways of handling the following situations and discuss the "strengths" and "weaknesses" of each method. Then construct a new response that you would consider to be more effective.

I.

During a private caucus one of the parties begins expressing insecurity about participating in the mediation. She describes a lack of trust in the other side and fears that revealing information now will cause her trouble in the future. She begins probing you for your take on the situation. She wants to know whose side you believe and she directly asks for your opinion.

In response to her probing you state: "I'm really not in a position to judge this situation. I think I understand your fears and I can pose some of your concerns to the other side. I believe things are going well so far; why don't we go forward and see what happens?"

1. What are the strengths of this response?
2. What are the weaknesses of this response?
3. Present a more effective response.

II.

After hearing the stories of both sides you begin to feel very sympathetic toward one of the parties. You not only believe that this side is right, but you also resent what you see as underhanded manipulation of a weaker person by the other side.

As a response to these strong feelings, you believe that you simply must take some action. During a caucus with the side you favor, you state: "I just have to tell you that I am appalled with what the other side is doing to you. You have every right to stand up for yourself—have you ever considered suing?"

1. What are the strengths of this response?
2. What are the weaknesses of this response?
3. Present a more effective response.

Consider these ideas:

- Participants in mediation have chosen this route. They want an impartial mediator.
- Demonstrating any alliance conveys that you cannot be trusted.
- Expressing emotional involvement suggests you cannot be objective.
- Empathy is impartial. It is acknowledging a person's feelings or beliefs as genuine.
- Sympathy is not impartial. It is supporting a person's feelings or beliefs as truth.
- A personal alliance with one side suggests the same will occur with the other side.
- Breaching impartiality expresses a lack of respect for the wishes of the participants.
- Breaching impartiality portrays incompetence.

Ethical Challenges

During mediation, situations may arise that challenge your beliefs and sense of "right and wrong." Mediators are not judges, but they do have opinions. At times you may find that you identify with one of the parties. You may even believe one side is truthful and the other is lying. There will be occasions when you find your sense of fairness and justice nagging. These times can be frustrating and confusing.

Consider the following situations. There is no single correct answer, but there may be clearly wrong answers. Remember, your job is not to police, it is to help resolve other peoples' problems.

I.

You are a mediator for a dispute between two employees. You have been trained by your company as a mediator for their in-house dispute resolution program. You are also a paid employee and a supervisor but do not work with either of the parties in this dispute. You were chosen by these parties because they knew your reputation for being impartial and maintaining confidentiality.

During the mediation you find out that one of the employees has been stealing small items on a regular basis. These items include things like office supplies, totaling around $100. It is not your job to police the office, but you do feel that stealing is a serious offense; if this person worked under you, it would be your job to fire them. Neither of the parties is a supervisor and it is unlikely anyone will find out about the stealing if you don't tell. You have taken an oath of confidentiality and impartiality that you take very seriously. You know that if people can't trust you to be impartial and keep their privacy, your reputation will be destroyed and the mediation program may fail.

1. You have just found out about the stealing directly from the person who stole. You are told about it in a private caucus. You are sitting alone in a room with this person when you hear the news. How do you respond?

2. You now switch sides and see the other party for a private caucus. You have this information weighing on your conscience, but the thief specifically told you the information was secret. What do you do?

3. The mediation is over. You are now in your normal role of supervisor, sitting in a meeting. The issue of employee theft comes up unexpectedly. There is talk around the table that stealing is costing the company money. The group is brainstorming. What do you reveal to the group?

4. You run into the company president in the hall. She knows about the mediation program and is curious about its success. She asks you how you like being a medi-

ator. Then she says, "I hope you're doing a good job of keeping our workers in line." How do you respond?

5. Consider how your choices will affect the people involved and the company as a whole. What are the positive results of your choices and what are the negative results?

6. How did your personal moral, ethical, and religious values affect your choices?

II.

You are still a mediator in the same firm. Most of the details are the same, except that instead of stealing, you find out that one party has been sexually harassing the other. The harassment involves propositions for sex, including descriptions of explicit sexual acts. The language used is rude and offensive, and also quite threatening. The person being threatened is beginning to fear for her safety. She is emotionally very upset. She even starts to cry.

To add to this terrible dilemma, she refuses to report the sexual harasser because he has seniority and is "in" with the boss. She fears that reporting him will only cause her more problems. She thinks it could possibly cost her the job.

1. You have just found out about the sexual harassment from the woman being harassed. You are told about it in a private caucus. You are sitting alone with this woman and as she tells you she begins to cry. How do you respond?

2. You now switch sides and see the other party for a private caucus. You have this information weighing on your conscience, but the woman specifically told you the information was secret. What do you do?

3. The mediation is over. You are now in your normal role of supervisor, sitting in a meeting. The issue of employee sexual harassment comes up unexpectedly. There is talk around the table about sexual harassment lawsuits and the new "no tolerance" policy. The group is brainstorming. What do you reveal to the group?

4. You run into the company president in the hall. She knows about the mediation program and is curious about its success. She asks you how you like being a mediator. Then she says, "I hope you're doing a good job of keeping our workers in line." How do you respond?

5. Consider how your choices will affect the people involved and the company as a whole. What are the positive results of your choices and what are the negative results?

6. How did your personal moral, ethical, and religious values affect your choices?

Issues in the Workplace

No one wants to be in the middle of a dispute. Conflict is stressful and often frightening; conflict at work is particularly difficult. With our family and friends we can expect to eventually "make up." The consequences of a personal conflict are usually not devastating. In a work situation conflict can be more serious—or at least feel more serious. Initiating mediation can be intimidating. People who come to mediation will have unexpressed concerns and reservations about the process.

Many factors will affect the success of mediation:

- The reason for the mediation.
- The personalities of the participants.
- The goals of the parties.
- Any hidden agendas.
- The ability of the participants to have a forthright and honest negotiation.
- The balance of power between the parties.
- Hidden fears and doubts about the process.
- The ability of the mediator.
- The level of trust formed between the mediator and the parties.
- And a host of unforeseen circumstances.

Read the following scenarios and answer the questions realistically. Consider that the ideal approach may not always be possible in real life. The goal of this exercise is to examine responses that are reasonable, practical, and effective.

I.

A conflict exists between a supervisor and a subordinate worker. The supervisor tends to be very demanding and sometimes offends her workers with harsh criticism. However, she genuinely respects her staff even though she has trouble showing it. She wants mediation to work, although she fears her workers don't trust her. The subordinate worker also wants mediation to work, but doesn't trust the boss. Secretly she fears retaliation and is overwhelmed by the stress of the whole situation. She is considering quitting her job to avoid any more conflict.

1. Discuss the obstacles you see that may make a mediation between these two people difficult.

2. Discuss the potential benefits of a successful mediation between these two people. Can the working relationship be improved by addressing some of the issues described?

Consider these questions:

- Will the supervisor's harsh and inconsiderate personality be intimidating?
- Will the worker be bullied because of her meek personality?
- How can the hidden respect the supervisor feels be drawn out?
- How can the worker be encouraged to participate despite her desire to give up?
- How can mediation prevent any retaliation?
- Will the lack of trust make honest communication impossible?
- How can both people feel supported and be empowered to speak out without fear?

Consider these possibilities:

- Sharing hidden information may build empathy and trust.
- An opportunity to ask direct questions may reduce suspicion and fear.
- The input of an outsider now may help to make communication easier in the future.
- Listening to another perspective may clear up mistaken perceptions.
- Learning the consequences of behavior may lead to more thoughtful behavior.
- Ending speculation by exposing true feelings may lessen defensiveness and stress.

II.

A conflict has arisen between two coworkers over dividing job responsibilities. Both coworkers have equal status jobs. Both are also hoping to get the one available promotion. The workers have the same job description and are required to divide all the work themselves. Some of the work done every day is very time-consuming, but not very challenging. The rest of the work is the "glamor" work; it is more interesting and often evokes praise from the boss. Each worker feels the other is trying to undermine him and take all the glamor work to impress the boss. In the meantime, little is getting done.

1. Discuss the obstacles you see that may make a mediation between these two people difficult.
2. Discuss the potential benefits of a successful mediation between these two people. Can the working relationship be improved by resolving some of the issues described?

Consider these questions:

- Will the competitive nature of the relationship be a barrier to any cooperation?
- Will the history of distrust hinder honest conversation?
- Can people compromise when both sides want something that only one can have?
- If an organization is structured to promote competition, is it wise to collaborate?
- Will revealing hidden intentions reduce competition?
- Is it fair to encourage a partnership when only one side may benefit in the end?

Consider these possibilities:

- Competitive relationships create a hostile environment that is unpleasant to work in.
- Lack of communication negatively affects all work.
- Assumptions about what is valued in the workplace may be incorrect.
- Collaboration could strengthen the entire department, creating more opportunities.
- Time wasted on hostility and suspicion detracts from work accomplishments.
- Teamwork is often considered important for overall success in the workplace.

III.

A worker files a discrimination claim against his employer. He believes he was not promoted because he is black. There is only one other black person in the organization (also never promoted). The organization supervisor claims that there was no discrimination and honestly believes this to be true. In fact, she has been intentionally interviewing minority workers for the open positions.

1. Discuss the obstacles you see that may make a mediation between these two people difficult.
2. Discuss the potential benefits of a successful mediation between these two people. Can the working relationship be improved by resolving some of these issues?

Consider these questions:

- Will personal or political convictions lead to an intolerance of other perspectives?
- Can an individual who feels betrayed accept an opposing explanation?
- If there are hidden agendas, will honest communication be possible?
- Will poor work performance be discussed if ignoring the issue is much easier?
- Should illegal activities be explored if accusations may destroy reputations?
- Will the fear of legal action provoke parties to distort information or lie?
- Will the desire to be vindicated provoke parties to distort information or lie?

Consider these possibilities:

- Personal and political convictions have led to misjudgments about ulterior motives.
- Ignorance about the history of inequality has resulted in callous insensitivity.
- Paranoia and fear have developed as a result of long-term lack of communication.
- Dissatisfaction with work has been concealed due to fears of recrimination.
- Work performance may never improve if no complaints are expressed.
- Inconsistent practices are sloppy but not necessarily intentional.
- Embarrassment or discomfort surrounding racial issues may hinder communication.

Part Two

Practice Concerns

Asking Questions

Read the following statements told to you by a participant during a caucus. Design questions that you would ask to draw out greater detail and challenge the preconceived ideas of the participant. Remember the concepts you have learned, such as impartiality and empathy. Also remember that the main purpose of asking questions is to reveal information, not to challenge the sincerity or veracity of the participant. You are assembling a story and your questions should be used to develop that story.

Pointer: New mediators often ask questions in a very direct and threatening manner. You are not a lawyer cross-examining a witness. Mediators are curious, cautious, and patient. Avoid phrasing questions so they sound like accusations. Be conscious of the tone of your voice. Don't demand information and don't sound exasperated when you don't get the answers you need right away.

Pointer: Let the information flow as naturally as possible. Listen carefully and use common sense. The questions and answers will come easily if you do not force or intimidate the speaker. You are just gathering information. Think of gathering information as a stroll down a road; questions are like pebbles that show up in your path—simply reach down and pick them up.

I.

"I have been working at this office for about a year. A new office manager just started and right from the start I did not like her. I just got a cold feeling from her. The old office manager and I were friends. We would have drinks after work sometimes. She would always come to me when an important decision had to be made and we would discuss it. The one time I went to this new office manager to get some details about an important project, she was polite, I guess, but didn't answer any questions. I have mentioned this to some of the other women in the office and they all agree, she is cold and difficult to work with. We have always had such a friendly office, but now this new woman, right out of the blue, asks for mediation. I talked to the other women and we all think she has problems."

1. Develop a list of questions.

II.

"I am the new office manager in the office; I took the job of a woman who worked here for eight years. I know I am good at my job and I enjoy it, but the atmosphere in the office is so tense you could cut it with a knife. I swear the other women stare at me when I walk down the hall and I know they are talking about me behind my back. I tried to make friends when I first got here, but the women were cold. Frankly, I don't care that much about making friends, but I don't understand why they dislike me so much. I am here to work not socialize. But the stress of knowing they resent me is affecting my work. When I started this job, the boss told me about the mediation process and I thought it was a great idea. I want to work things out but I worry that having asked for mediation will only make them hate me more."

1. Develop a list of questions.

Rephrasing and Reframing

Rephrasing is simply rewording a statement made by someone else in your own words. The words you use are yours, but they will convey the same meaning and spirit of the original statement.

Reframing is a translation or redefining. In reframing, the general idea of the message is communicated, but the language is changed in such a way that the spirit or feeling is altered.

Rephrase each statement using your own words to express the same idea. Remember that the purpose of rephrasing is to demonstrate a comprehension of the facts and also a sensitivity toward the spirit and intent of the message, showing empathy with the speaker.

Reframe each statement. The purpose of reframing is to make a comment sound more tactful and sympathetic and less critical, often by either de-emphasizing or emphasizing the emotional content. Reframing is also a way to help a person gain objectivity and discover new ways of perceiving a situation. It helps the person to reevaluate the intent of the message and the potential consequences of sending that message.

Consider these suggestions:

- Overemphasizing negative messages may foster a sense of hopelessness.
- Placing blame may trigger a defensive response and create barriers.
- Overdramatizing emotion may cue the listener that feelings expressed are irrational.
- Expressing extreme anger may trigger a defensive response.
- Avoid conveying embarrassing or humiliating statements.
- Present statements as objectively as possible without losing the meaning and intent.
- Attempt to empathize with both sides when choosing words that rephrase or reframe.
- Attempt to build a more positive message into the reworded statements.

I.

"I am furious at the constant lack of respect here. He thinks he owns me and can order me around like a dog."

1. Rephrase.
2. Reframe.

II.

"These workers are simply lazy and shiftless. I have a business to run here. You would think it was a country club not an office, the way they come and go as they please."

1. Rephrase.
2. Reframe.

III.

"You can tell him that I will not move one inch toward raising his salary if he doesn't start pulling his weight by putting in the hours that I do."

1. Rephrase.
2. Reframe.

IV.

"Please explain to me what the big deal is. I have no problem with the work 'environment,' as she would put it. I am just doing my job; I don't take these things very seriously."

1. Rephrase.
2. Reframe.

V.

"Every night I go home and cry myself to sleep, I am so stressed out. But don't tell her that—she loves making my life miserable."

1. Rephrase.
2. Reframe.

VI.

"Look, do we have to keep yammering about this crap; let's just get down to business and cut a deal. I'm ready if he's ready, let's move it along."

1. Rephrase.
2. Reframe.

VII.

"Screw this. I'm calling my lawyer."

1. Rephrase.
2. Reframe.

Dealing with Emotion

Different people have unique reactions to stressful situations. Despite all the attempts to make mediation a nonthreatening experience, the participants will still experience stress. Unfortunately, the state of being "stressed-out" is not the most conducive to rational problem solving. It is the mediator's job to help the participants get through the distracting moments and focus on the real work of resolving problems.

Consider the following scenarios. Mediators have to react in an appropriately sensitive fashion during any type of emotional outburst. Evaluate the proposed ways of handling the following situations and discuss the "strengths" and "weaknesses" of the method. Then construct what you would consider an effective response.

Pointer: One of the benefits of mediation is that the participants have the opportunity to express feelings and vent frustrations. Often, simply getting pent-up emotion off your chest is an important first step to resolving a conflict. However, dwelling on emotion is not productive; mediation is not therapy and the mediator must set boundaries.

I.

During a mediation one of the participants breaks down into tears and begins to talk about her troubles at home. Obviously her personal suffering is affecting her interactions with others, but it does not directly relate to the issues of the mediation.

Allow her to cry and tell her story during the caucus. Then guide her back to the issues of the mediation.

1. What are the strengths of this response?
2. What are the weaknesses of this response?
3. Present a more effective response.

Consider these ideas:

- Empathizing is a good way to build trust.
- Venting emotional pain can relieve stress.
- Permitting expressions of vulnerability may diminish defensive or hostile behavior.
- Strong emotions can be distracting.

- Sympathizing may appear to be an expression of "taking sides."
- Overwhelming situations that cannot be controlled will disrupt the process.

II.

During a mediation one of the participants begins to get very hostile. First he makes several snide remarks, which everyone ignores. Finally he stands up and yells: "I can't stand this bullshit anymore."

In a very strong and authoritarian voice you state: "Please sit down and control yourself, language like that is inappropriate and offensive."

1. What are the strengths of this response?
2. What are the weaknesses of this response?
3. Present a more effective response.

Consider these ideas:

- Inappropriate outbursts may be uncontrolled ways of expressing useful information.
- Emotion is expressed in different forms by different people.
- Extreme anger may be a sign of feeling overwhelmed.
- Inappropriate outbursts may intimidate and manipulate, silencing others.
- Assertiveness and aggression are interpreted differently.
- Demonstrating respect is more effective than demanding it.
- People tend to take social cues from those in charge.
- Never push someone to the breaking-point.
- Threatening or dangerous behavior is a cue to end the process.

Dealing with Lying

Despite the promise that the participants make to engage in open and honest negotiations, on occasion people will lie. Lying is not always intended to be destructive; often it is a self-protective response. Disputes can grow from actions that people later regret and make them feel ashamed. Often, conflict results from irresponsible or inconsiderate behavior. In these cases, lying may be a way to mask shame. Certainly, people also lie in an attempt to manipulate and gain some desired outcome. The motivation for a lie will probably impact which method is most effective for responding to it during mediation.

Consider the following scenarios. Mediators have to react in an appropriate fashion when confronted with lying. Evaluate the proposed ways of handling the following situations and discuss the "strengths" and "weaknesses" of the method. Then construct what you would consider an effective response.

Pointer: One lie does not necessarily define the behavior of a person. When you recognize that a lie has been told, attempt to view that lie in the context of patterns you have seen. A person who has been consistently deceptive or evasive may have different motivations than the person who makes an unbelievable statement "out of the blue." Viewing the person as a whole may help you determine the most effective way to break down this barrier.

I.

You notice that one of the participants has made several statements that clearly contradict each other. You can't tell if the person is deliberately lying or is confused. But you suspect the person is hiding something important. With permission, you have inadvertently passed some of this muddled information to the other side.

In response to this troubling realization you state: "You have made some statements that confuse me. Could you help clear up this problem I have? It is very important that I understand the situation clearly and accurately."

1. What are the strengths of this response?
2. What are the weaknesses of this response?
3. Present a more effective response.

II.

During a private caucus you realize that one of the parties has definitely been lying. You suspect that if these lies become known, they will destroy the work that has been accomplished so far.

In response to this troubling realization you state: "I feel I have to say that your story is quite different from the one I heard from the other side. I think it is very important that everyone be truthful during this process or there is little point in continuing. Don't you agree?"

1. What are the strengths of this response?
2. What are the weaknesses of this response?
3. Present a more effective response.

Consider these ideas:

• Lies may be a way to cover uncomfortable or embarrassing information.
• Lies may simply be attempts to manipulate.
• Direct confrontation may be effective, particularly if the liar wants to be caught.
• Direct confrontation may be humiliating and destroy trust.
• Probing for answers with nonthreatening questions may draw out information.
• Probing for answers may do little more than trick a liar into admitting the truth.
• Probing for answers may frighten or anger a person and exacerbate lying.
• Probing for answers with threatening questions may evoke a confession.

Confidentiality Concerns

Learning to maintain confidentiality about secrets while simultaneously revealing information that the party wishes to share is probably the most critical mediator skill. Revealing confidential information is also the act that leaves both the parties and the mediator most vulnerable. Virtually any other mistake can be mended. But once a secret has been revealed, it cannot be unexposed. There is nothing a mediator can do that is more destructive than breaching confidentiality. It not only destroys the mediation, but it can directly harm the participants.

The most volatile information, the big secrets, are usually obvious; this is also the information that comes with specific instructions. It is the more subtle information that can trip up a mediator. A mediator will most likely breach confidentiality by exposing some minor point that just slips out. A breach of confidentiality is usually an accident—and a surprise.

Consider the following scenarios about confidentiality dilemmas. Evaluate the proposed ways of handling the following situations and discuss the "strengths" and "weaknesses" of each method. Then construct what you would consider an effective response.

I.

After returning from a private caucus with the "other side," you are accused of revealing private information. The participant says to you: "You knew that was private information, I specifically told you not to mention it. Did you or didn't you tell my secret?" In this case, you did not.

You respond very calmly: "I did understand that was private information and I did not share it. I don't want you to be uncomfortable anticipating what I might say; why don't I review everything with you first, before I speak with the other side again?"

1. What are the strengths of this response?
2. What are the weaknesses of this response?
3. Present a more effective response.

Consider these ideas:

- Being excluded from important discussions may lead to anxiousness and suspicion.
- Reassurance is an important tool for building trust.

- Patience demonstrates respect.
- Honest evaluations are generally appreciated, even if the truth is discomforting.
- Condescending attitudes are universally destructive.
- Hostility is normally destructive.
- Defensive responses are more likely to heighten apprehensions then reassure.

II.

During a caucus you have learned a very important piece of information that would probably settle the dispute. When you mention this to the party, she responds: "Yeah, it may settle the dispute, but it would ruin my life."

Somewhat shocked at her statement, you say: "That's a little dramatic, don't you think? Why don't you give me a chance to run it by the other side? I'm sure everything will be fine."

1. What are the strengths of this response?
2. What are the weaknesses of this response?
3. Present a more effective response.

Consider these ideas:

- Tactful critique is an essential skill to master.
- The parties control the flow of information.
- Commentary perceived as a personal affront will offend and create barriers.
- Judgmental responses rarely serve a productive purpose.
- Tactful, yet critical evaluations will generally be well received.

III.

During a private caucus that seems to be going just fine, you let a piece of secret information slip out, to your great surprise. It was really the way you worded the statement that was revealing. If you had just said it a little differently, there would have been no problem.

You respond by saying: "Let me backtrack here. I think I described that wrong. I don't want you to get the wrong impression; sometimes when I carry information back and forth, I let my personal interpretation affect the translation."

1. What are the strengths of this response?
2. What are the weaknesses of this response?
3. Present a more effective response.

Consider these ideas:

- Listeners take cues about how to interpret information from the speaker.
- Using tact to avoid causing harm is not deceitful.
- Portraying uncertainty will alarm the listener.
- If the speaker does not believe the statement, the listener certainly will not.
- "The truth" will have varying interpretations.
- Interpretations of facts, which are perceived as reasonable, are likely to be believed.

IV.

When you return to the side whose secret you revealed, you say: "Look, I made a major mistake. I don't want to scare you, but I think I may really have messed up. I told the other side this really important piece of information that I know you wanted to keep a secret. What do you want me to do now?"

1. What are the strengths of this response?
2. What are the weaknesses of this response?
3. Present a more effective response.

Consider these ideas:

- Overly dramatic explanations may generate fear or distrust.
- Expressing negative scenarios in the least threatening manner is less destructive.
- Suggesting that others repair your mistakes breeds resentment.
- Use restraint when choosing words to explain threatening information.
- Use sensitivity when choosing words to explain painful or frightening information.
- Consider the consequences of your words before you speak.

Part Three

Mock Mediations

Mock Mediations

The following scenarios are to be used for practice mediation. It is essential that any new mediator practice several times before attempting the real thing. It may also be useful for a new mediator to experience the role of participant. These role-play mediations can be repeated with the participants switching roles. Different people will bring very different characters to each role, making the experience of each interaction unique.

Mock mediation should be performed as if it were a genuine mediation. Nevertheless it is appropriate, and often very useful, for the players to give each other feedback and advice during the process. Having a nonparticipant watch and critique is also a valuable exercise. The ideal training scenario is to employ an experienced mediator to critique the process, evaluate technique, and offer suggestions.

INSTRUCTIONS

1. These mock mediations require at least three players: the mediator and two participants, the parties.

2. Each mock mediation contains both "public" and "private" information. Both parties must read the pages labeled public information; the mediator can choose whether or not to read it. This is the information that will be shared during the participant opening remarks.

3. Only the person playing the particular role (for instance, Tina) may read the private information for that character. The mediator may not read any of the private information. This is information that will be shared during caucusing.

4. The people playing the parties should feel free to embellish these stories, as long as the scenario remains realistic. The gender of each role can be changed whenever necessary.

Sally and Bob

SALLY AND BOB: PUBLIC INFORMATION

Sally and Bob both work for a public service agency. The agency is large and has offices around the state. Each office has a manager who supervises around ten employees. Sally is the manager and Bob is a social service worker who works directly with clients. Sally does mostly administrative work, although she occasionally works with clients. At the job site Sally is the direct supervisor and her staff addresses most issues with her. However, Sally does have two supervisors above her who regularly request work updates. Sally's staff is not really aware of how often she talks with her supervisors and how much they know. Sally is basically a fair boss, but she is more of an administrator than a "people person" and often has trouble communicating with her staff. Sally has a B.A. in Accounting and Office Management and has been working at the agency for fifteen years.

Bob is a very caring and sensitive person who started working at the agency six months ago. He was hired because he has a Masters Degree in Social Work (MSW) and an excellent reputation for working with clients. Being a people person, he loves to talk and this often includes office gossip. None of Bob's coworkers have graduate degrees but all have been at the agency much longer than Bob. When Bob started work, the feelings in the office were mixed. Although they were glad to have such an educated person around, they were worried about their own job security and a little resentful of the extra money Bob would make.

There are several conflicts going on here. First of all, Bob recently stormed into Sally's office and said: "I am so tired of being the only one who actually helps clients around here, I need a serious raise if you want to keep me." Sally was taken aback and slightly overwhelmed. It is true that her agency does not pay MSW workers as well as some other agencies, but Bob does make more money that any other social service worker in the office. Sally does not like conflict to begin with, and to make matters worse she knew several other workers could hear Bob yelling his demands. Her response to Bob was: "I can't talk to you now—come back later." Bob then stormed out. Sally has been avoiding Bob for several weeks and in the meantime Bob has been "mentioning" this conversation all around the office. Bob then files for mediation.

SALLY: PRIVATE INFORMATION

Several minutes after Bob stormed out of the office, the workers who overheard the yelling came in to see Sally. They were mad. They couldn't believe what an arrogant jerk Bob was. "Who does he think he is; we have been here ten times longer than that know-it-all." Again Sally avoided the confrontation by listening but giving no response. Bob never knew this happened.

On the other hand, Bob actually does perform superior work and Sally is getting tremendous pressure from her bosses to hire only MSW workers and then keep them. There actually may be money for a raise for Bob, but he is such a big mouth that everyone will find out about it. Sally dreads the anger and hostility by her workers when they find out. To add to this mess her bosses have been hinting that "getting rid of" non-MSW workers may be good for the organization since the state gives more grant money for MSWs. None of Sally's workers know this.

The other problem is that her bosses have been giving Sally a hard time for her tendency to avoid conflict with her staff. She regularly neglects to do performance evaluations and Bob's is past due. In her evaluation of Bob she must tell him that he is an excellent social service worker, but she also must reprimand him for his terrible interpersonal skills at the office. Bob has no idea about this.

BOB: PRIVATE INFORMATION

The day that Bob stormed into Sally's office he had just been offered a job at another agency for much more money. No one at the office even thought he was looking for a new job. However, unfortunately for Bob, the next day he found out that the funding was denied and he didn't have the job after all. He was quite nervous about what he had done; he knew it was a bad move and regretted it now. That is why he has been avoiding Sally.

On the other hand, he knows he is a great social service worker and does feel he deserves more money. He could always look for a better job. He felt very tense at the office, Sally never gave him any feedback, and he resented that he still had not been given a performance evaluation. His way of dealing with Sally was to hint at things to his coworkers. He was just trying to "feel things out." After all, Sally never talked to him and he felt the resentment of his coworkers like a knife. He was under a lot of stress and was the new guy everyone hated, and so he just exploded. Bob would really like to work things out—he likes the job and his clients—but feels over his head with the other pressures. If he can't get a raise, he really may look for another job.

George and Tina

GEORGE AND TINA: PUBLIC INFORMATION

George and Tina work for a medium-size company that George started twenty-five years ago and built from the ground up. George is the president and very proud of his business; it is his whole life. He is also very protective and thinks of the company as his "baby," a phrase he often uses at meetings. George has the attitude that working for his "baby" is an honor and a privilege. He comes from the "old school," where a worker is a worker and a boss is a boss. That is not to say he doesn't reward his employees; the pay is good and the benefits are great. He expects total commitment from his workers and in return he offers job security for life. He prides himself on being in control and in charge. He is like the father of his company.

Tina is George's personal secretary. She has been working for him for five years. Tina is a top-notch secretary, and the perfect employee for George. To begin with, she never calls him by his first name. She is quiet and subservient; she does what she is told and does it well. From the outside everything appears great. The only problem is that George has a tendency to use language that is slightly old-fashioned. He calls Tina "honey" and "sweetheart." Tina has tolerated this. But lately George has been requiring Tina to stay late at the office and she has noticed that he touches her a lot. Although she has said nothing, Tina is upset and also a little scared.

The grievance policy at the company has always been very simple. If you have a complaint, present it to George and he will make an executive decision. However, several months ago, for no apparent reason, George implemented an in-house mediation procedure with peer mediators and complicated rules. So far no one has dared to use it. It has come as a tremendous surprise to everyone, but all of a sudden Tina has filed a grievance against George. Everyone knows that George is absolute about rules, and the plan has compliance rules that assure no retaliation, so no one fears that they will lose their jobs. But this is a new experience for everyone.

GEORGE: PRIVATE INFORMATION

George has been under a great deal of pressure lately. The company is doing very well financially, but this increase in business has made George's workload unbearable. His familiar style of being the "do everything" boss isn't working anymore. His employees are becoming more independent, but this is hard for George to take. His usual response to employee autonomy is to become more authoritarian, more bossy. He is also used to hiring and firing whom he wants, when he wants. Recently two of his former workers filed lawsuits against him and his company. One was for sex discrimination and one was for wrongful termination. The mediation policy was his lawyer's suggestion, a new young lawyer with modern ideas. However, with all the problems in the company George was receptive and genuinely intends to give mediation a try.

The grievance Tina filed against him came as a complete shock. He always thought of Tina as a good worker, and a "good girl." He is not so much angry as scared. His wife recently left him, claiming he was overbearing and tried to "own" her. He simply thought he was acting like a husband was supposed to. He has to admit (but only to himself) that he is lonely and does find Tina attractive. Maybe he was hoping something would happen, but he never meant to hurt her. He doesn't want another lawsuit, and he also doesn't want to lose Tina as a secretary. His lawyer told him that if Tina files a lawsuit she could win a great deal of money and damage the company reputation. On the other hand, he is the boss and will not tolerate employee insubordination; what he says goes.

TINA: PRIVATE INFORMATION

It took more courage than Tina ever thought she had to file her grievance and she is terrified. She likes her job and most of the time she likes George, but she feels threatened and humiliated when he makes advances and calls her "honey." She has known all along that he wasn't supposed to do those things, but never had the guts to stand up to him. Workers don't stand up to George. Her courage came from having a friend at another company who filed a sexual harassment suit against her boss and won $250,000. It was not just the money that motivated her, she also learned a great deal about her rights. But the money was tempting too.

When Tina got this job right out of school she was led to believe she could work there for the rest of her life, and that is just what she wanted. She thought she could tolerate George's little remarks, but now the situation is out of control. The other problem for her is that there are no other jobs in the area that pay as well and she cannot afford to take a pay cut. Also, she needs her medical benefits; she has a chronic medical problem and even with her good benefits she barely makes ends meet. No one at work knows about her health problems. Although she cannot afford to lose her job, she has already decided that she will stand up to George and not let him intimidate her. If she has to, she will sue him in court.

Frank and Bill

FRANK AND BILL: PUBLIC INFORMATION

Frank and Bill are real estate agents at a successful real estate firm. The firm is a franchise operated by Bill's mother and owned by a large corporate enterprise. Several of Bill's family members also work at the firm. Although agents share listings of properties and occasionally show each other's houses, they are paid on commission.

Recently, a large company has closed in town and many people have moved away. There has been a dramatic increase of houses on the market and a decrease in sales. Competition in the office has become somewhat fierce, although no one discusses it publicly. Everyone has been working harder lately and there is a palatable stress in the office.

Bill is a competent salesman and committed to the overall success of the firm. His style is easygoing and low pressure, but he does have a temper that flairs when he suspects questionable ethical practices. He has been in the business for many years and has seen quite a few agents use underhanded selling techniques. Bill knows from experience that a slump in the market is a time when agents tend to take desperate risks; he is not shy about reminding his colleagues of this. His philosophy, which he frequently states publicly, is: "A man with honor and a mission will always ride out the rough seas of life."

Frank is a much more aggressive salesman than Bill. He spends a great deal of time with his clients socializing to forward his career. He has the best sales record in the firm and makes the most money of any salesman. Frank is ambitious and would like to own his own firm one day. He knows he has no chance of owning this firm because it will stay in Bill's family. He is not particularly concerned with the firm's reputation, although he is concerned with his own. He has a five-year plan to save enough money for his own business, but the slump in the market is putting quite a crimp in his plans.

Recently, Frank has sold two houses to buyers who were originally Bill's clients. "Stealing clients" is not only against firm policy, but considered a "sin" in the office. Occasionally agents "trade" or "share" clients and split the commission. In this case Frank met the clients while socializing at the country club. He didn't know they were Bill's clients first, but, then again, he didn't ask.

Bill discussed the conflict with Frank, who was apologetic. But Bill could not dismiss the issue and began to grow more and more angry. He started to discuss the issue with his family members in the firm privately, who all agreed that Frank must be "plotting to rip off more houses." Bill went to his mother and insisted that she fire Frank. She refused because Frank brings in the most money for the firm, and she also knows about Bill's tendency to get morally outraged at little things. She suspects that Frank is probably not the most honorable agent, but, in this market, she is willing to live with it. Unfortunately, the office is getting quite tense, with a division between the family members and the other employees at the firm. Bill's mother has decided to call in a mediator from the corporation that owns the firm to help resolve the dispute.

FRANK: PRIVATE INFORMATION

There is more going on behind the scenes then Frank has let on. Frank has recently taken out a bank loan because of some private matters that no one at the firm knows about. He has been unable to make the monthly payments because of the slow sales. If his credit rating is ruined, he will never get a loan to open his own firm in the next few years.

Although he didn't actually know that those questionable house sales were to Bill's clients, he suspected they might be and intentionally did not look at the files. To make matters worse, he was recently approached by the owner of the country club who is planning to sell many properties in the near future. The country club owner offered to let Frank personally represent all his properties if Frank gives him a percentage of the commission. This sort of kickback is illegal in the state and Frank could lose his real estate license and his job, or worse. On the other hand, it would solve all his financial problems. He has not accepted the offer—yet.

Frank has also been secretly approached by Bill's mother. She is pleased with his selling style and his number of sales. She let him know that his sales are carrying the firm right now and she would hate to lose him. He was flattered by the compliment, but when he asked for a larger commission, she said that it could not be done right now. She did say that if he stuck around, there was a very good chance for "advancement" in the firm. Frank is not sure exactly what that means.

BILL: PRIVATE INFORMATION

Bill is having more troubles at work than anyone knows. His mother and he have never gotten along very well. She pressured him into joining the firm and since then she has pressured him to change his selling style. The only thing that makes selling real estate bearable for him is the easygoing style and the many afternoons he takes off to play golf.

Although he is concerned about the reputation of the firm, his obsession with ethics has a lot to do with keeping the firm selling style low-pressure, which will keep his mother off his back. Right now the rest of his family supports him, but he worries that, with sales so slow, they will begin to side with his mother and insist on high-pressure selling.

His problems with Frank started long before the client "stealing" incident. He knows his mother likes Frank's style and he fears that Frank will influence the rest of the family, especially now that he is keeping the firm afloat. He also has a secret that no one knows. In private, he is relieved that his mother is so fond of Frank. He has been wanting to quit the firm for years but hasn't had the courage. Part of him is trying to build enough tension in the office so that his mother will fire him. Of course he can't tell Frank that his ethical outrage is mostly for show, to keep his family on his side. The truth is, his biggest fear is that Frank will quit and Bill will be stuck in the firm forever. He feels like he is stuck between a rock and a hard place.

Section III

PROGRAM IMPLEMENTATION

An in-house mediation program will assist employees to resolve on-the-job conflict with the help of fellow workers. The following sections include the administrative tools necessary to implement a workplace peer mediation program. Individual organizations may want to customize aspects of the plan to suit their specific needs.

For best results, an organization should officially incorporate the mediation plan into personnel policy. The plan must be introduced as a formal and accepted mechanism for resolving disputes. Employers should consider how the plan will be promoted and advertised within the organization. An important part of implementing a mediation policy is building trust with the employees; for this to be accomplished, commitment to mediation must be evident from the outset.

The mediation program can be used by employees any time there is a conflict at work. Mediation is meant to be used before the dispute becomes so heated that a formal grievance—or, in the worst case scenario, a lawsuit—is filed. Mediation can also be used for serious disputes in place of a formal grievance, here again thwarting more drastic action. Mediation, commonly called "alternative dispute resolution," is also preventive dispute resolution.

In the workplace, expressing emotion is generally not acceptable. At home a small argument can be a useful way to vent frustrations and share ideas. At work, arguments are avoided and small annoyances can blossom into serious personnel problems. Mediation is an opportunity to express professional and sometimes emotional concerns in an appropriate setting.

In mediation the two (or more) disputing individuals meet with an impartial third party mediator. The mediator is not a judge and will only assist the individuals in coming to their own fair and mutually acceptable solution. One individual can apply for a mediation session, but every participant must agree to take part before the mediation will go forward.

Mediation is a voluntary process. This highlights the importance of trust in the workplace. If employees are suspicious of the sincerity of the employer, they will not volunteer to participate.

Disputes for Mediation

Any serious dispute that leads to dissatisfaction on the job is appropriate for mediation. Day-to-day interpersonal squabbles are appropriate for mediation when they affect work relationships. This process should be used freely, but not abused. Participants have the right to determine what is a "serious" dispute. People will have different interpretations about what causes conflict and stress on the job. All mediation must be initiated in good faith, with the intention of finding a resolution. Unless obviously frivolous, no request for mediation should be denied on the grounds that the conflict is silly or inconsequential.

In the unlikely occurrence that a serious question arises about whether an issue is appropriate for mediation, the Mediation Oversight Committee (MOC) has the sole discretion to make a determination. The MOC should not deny mediation because the behavior in question is prohibited by formal organization policy, such as dangerous or inappropriate activity, unless the conduct does not cease immediately after notification of the policy. The MOC may deny mediation for issues in which the behavior in question is prohibited by law, such as discriminatory or criminal activity. However, the MOC must recognize that a suspicion or accusation of criminal activity is in no way proof of that activity.

Mediation issues might include but are not limited to:

1. Consistent dissatisfaction with work performance.
2. Suspected unfair treatment or a feeling of discrimination.
3. Salary or benefit disputes.
4. Consistent interpersonal conflict that affects work performance or morale.
5. Harsh or unjust treatment by supervisors.
6. Insubordination by employees.
7. Employee abuses of the personnel policy guidelines, such as excessive sick leave without reasonable explanation.
8. Supervisory refusal to adhere to personnel policy guidelines, such as declining sick leave and vacation requests without reasonable explanation.
9. Harassment or threats of any kind.
10. Any other serious offense or dispute between employees that affects work performance or morale.

Mediation Oversight Committee

The Mediation Oversight Committee (MOC) is the democratic governing body and overseer of the mediation process. The MOC is the group of individuals responsible for monitoring the mediation process to ensure fairness, ethical behavior, and adherence to the rules. The MOC must evaluate and approve all adjustments to the mediation process. Any complaints regarding the mediation process will be addressed by the MOC. The MOC is the only rule-making authority and the only group charged with the power to issue reprimands or enact punitive measures. The MOC is the model for all conduct. Members of the MOC are held to the strictest standards and will adhere to all the rules and restrictions of the mediation process at all times.

DESIGN

1. Membership on the Mediation Oversight Committee is voluntary. Members of the MOC have significant power and responsibility. Full commitment to the role of MOC member is necessary for an effective and just mediation process; the success of the mediation process hinges on employee trust in the MOC.

2. MOC members must meet all the training and competency requirements set by the training program and the Mediation Oversight Committee.

3. The MOC will consist of three (3) voting members and one alternate.

4. The initial MOC will be appointed by either the mediation trainer or democratic popular vote. Candidates must meet the position requirements described below. MOC members will be selected based on competency and interest.

5. Replacement MOC members will be appointed through a democratic voting process. Each sitting member of the MOC and each member of the Board of Mediators has one vote. Majority rules. MOC members will be selected based on competency and interest.

6. One (1) voting member and the alternate will be selected from the Board of Directors. One (1) voting member will be selected from middle management. One (1) voting member will be selected from nonmanagement staff.

7. The alternate will participate in MOC meetings only when a voting member is unavailable. When participating, the alternate acts as a voting member.

8. Each MOC voting member has one (1) equal vote. Organization hierarchy does not apply with respect to MOC business.

9. Majority rules. All MOC decisions require three (3) votes.

10. If an MOC member is a party in mediation, or a complaint is filed against an MOC member, he or she cannot participate in MOC meetings regarding that case.

11. A member of the MOC cannot simultaneously serve on the Board of Mediators.

Board of Mediators

The Board of Mediators (BOM) is the group of individuals trained to act as peer mediators. The role of the mediator is to facilitate communication and assist the parties in reaching a mutually acceptable agreement. The mediator must remain impartial at all times. The mediator does not act in the capacity of a lawyer or a judge and does not offer legal advice or legal representation. The mediator is expected to act as a role model and will be held to the strictest standard of behavior.

DESIGN

1. Membership on the Board of Mediators is voluntary. BOM members must willingly accept the responsibility of participation. Uninterested or uncomfortable mediators will only hinder the mediation process.

2. BOM members must meet all the training and competency requirements set by the training program and the Mediation Oversight Committee.

3. The BOM will consist of ten (10) members.

4. The initial Board of Mediators will be appointed by either the mediation trainer or democratic popular vote. Candidates will be evenly distributed to represent management and nonmanagement jobs. BOM members will be selected based on competency and interest.

5. Replacement BOM members will be appointed by the Mediation Oversight Committee with input from sitting BOM members. BOM members will be selected based on competency and interest.

6. The BOM will consist of members who have diverse positions and levels of responsibility within the organization. Membership will be evenly distributed to represent management and nonmanagement jobs. Board of Directors members may serve on the Board of Mediators.

7. A member of the BOM cannot simultaneously serve on the Mediation Oversight Committee.

Procedural Rules

PR1. Any employee(s) can request a mediation by contacting the "Mediation Liaison" and completing a "Mediation Request Form." Mediation may not be requested in order to threaten or intimidate.

PR2. Duplicates of the request form will be sent to the individuals named as parties in the dispute. Any individual who has a unique position or "side" of the dispute is a "party."

PR3. After receiving the request, all the parties must contact the Mediation Liaison within one work week.

PR4. The organization encourages participation. However, the mediation process is voluntary. No one will be penalized for refusing to participate in mediation. Any party may refuse to mediate subject to the following criteria:

1. A subordinate worker named as a party may refuse to participate for any reason.

2. A worker in a superior position may refuse to participate for any acceptable reason. There is a presumption that a superior worker will agree to participate; it is the worker's responsibility to justify a refusal. The determination of whether a refusal is reasonable is determined by the Mediation Oversight Committee.

A superior worker can be required to attempt mediation, but will not be punished for an unsuccessful session pursued in good faith.

PR5. The Mediation Liaison will send a list of available mediators to all parties. This Board of Mediators will consist of impartial trained mediators from both management and nonmanagement positions.

PR6. Each party will select three (3) mediators from the Board of Mediators. The Mediation Liaison will appoint a mediator who was commonly selected by all parties, repeating the selection process as necessary to find a match. If the parties cannot agree on a mediator, the Mediation Oversight Committee may recommend that an outside mediator be sought.

PR7. The Mediation Liaison will schedule a mediation time and location that is acceptable to all involved. All mediation will be scheduled during work hours if possible. If mediation extends beyond work hours, organization rules for overtime or comp-time applies. Travel expenses will be reimbursed in accordance with organization policy for work-time activities.

PR8. Mediation can be expected to require three to five hours; however, there is no time limit. If mediation requires an additional session, the parties may schedule this session independently, confirming the date with the Mediation Liaison.

PR9. Prior to commencing mediation, all participants must read and sign an agreement to mediate. Each participant will receive a copy of this agreement.

PR10. Mediation may be terminated with a consensus that the session is not productive. There is no penalty to the parties for a mediation that has failed.

PR11. Participating in mediation does not preclude any person from using an alternative grievance procedure or the legal system if the dispute is not mutually resolved. Mediation can be attempted during a formal grievance process. If mediation is unsuccessful, the formal process will continue at the point at which it was halted with no penalty.

PR12. If any resolutions are generated during the mediation, a memorandum of agreement must be drafted. This document should include a detailed account of all the pertinent information needed to understand and comply with the agreement. Each participant will receive a copy of this memorandum.

PR13. To finalize mediation, a party confidentiality statement must be completed and signed by all the participants. This statement, part of the memorandum of agreement, must outline any issues that the parties agree to make public. All discussions and resolutions must be kept completely confidential, unless specific exceptions are made in writing. Each participant will receive a copy of this agreement.

PR14. All documentation regarding mediation will be returned to the parties. No written record of mediation will be held in any employee personnel file.

PR15. Any individual has the right to file a confidential complaint with the Mediation Oversight Committee. A complaint should only be filed as a last resort, when the mediation process has failed. All complaints to the MOC must be in writing, explaining the problem in detail. The MOC will arrange a private meeting to hear the complaint and response. The MOC will make a determination based on the information provided. The MOC can and should offer creative and nonpunitive options for resolving the complaint. All punitive action taken by the MOC must be made in accordance with the Mediation Disciplinary Guidelines.

PR16. The Mediation Oversight Committee may maintain separate private files containing information on issues before the MOC.

Compliance Rules

CR1. The purpose of mediation is to empower the participants with the tools to find mutually acceptable resolutions to disputes. The participants are free to explore issues as they see fit and are encouraged to design and implement creative solutions. The organization and all participants will support this mission to the fullest extent possible.

CR2. The Mediation Oversight Committee (MOC) is the democratic governing body and overseer of the mediation process. The MOC is the group of individuals responsible for monitoring the mediation process to ensure fairness, ethical behavior, and adherence to the rules. The MOC must evaluate and approve all adjustments to the mediation process. Any complaints regarding the mediation process will be addressed by the MOC. The MOC is the only rule-making authority and the only group charged with the power to issue reprimands or enact punitive measures. The MOC is the model for all standards and conduct. Members of the MOC will adhere to all the rules and restrictions of the mediation process at all times.

CR3. All peer mediators serve on the Board of Mediators. The role of the mediator is to facilitate communication and assist the parties in reaching a mutually acceptable agreement. The mediator must remain impartial at all times. The mediator does not act in the capacity of a lawyer or a judge and does not offer legal advice or legal representation. The mediator will be held to the strictest standard of behavior.

CR4. The parties in mediation are expected to negotiate in good faith and discuss all issues openly and honestly. The mediation process must never be used to take unfair advantage of another person.

CR5. Under no circumstances may any member of the organization, regardless of position, use the mediation process to intimidate, harass, threaten, manipulate, or harm the reputation of a person. Violation of this rule is subject to review by the Mediation Oversight Committee.

CR6. No information obtained from mediation will be used by the employer or any employee to reprimand or punish.

The following exceptions apply:

1. Consequences for behavior prohibited by law, such as discriminatory or criminal activity, will be dictated by established organization policy.

2. The Mediation Oversight Committee has discretion regarding behavior prohibited by formal organization policy, such as dangerous or inappropriate activity, only if the conduct does not cease immediately after a mediation agreement has been reached.

CR7. All information shared during the mediation process will remain confidential. The mediator must agree not to share any information with the employer or any employee of the organization. All notes taken by the mediator will be destroyed or be privately held by the mediator and will never be included in employee personnel files.

The following exceptions to mediator confidentiality apply:

1. The mediator may reveal information related to behavior prohibited by law, such as discriminatory or criminal activity, according to organization policy.
2. All information required by court order will not be treated as confidential. The mediator may reveal the information necessary to defend against a formal complaint filed with the Mediation Oversight Committee or a judicial authority.

CR8. All information shared during the mediation process will remain confidential. The parties must agree not to share any information with the employer or any employees of the organization.

The following exceptions to party confidentiality apply:

1. Public information may be shared as described in the party confidentiality statement.
2. Any party may reveal information related to behavior prohibited by law, such as discriminatory or criminal activity, according to organization policy.
3. Any party may reveal to the Mediation Oversight Committee information related to behavior prohibited by formal organization policy, such as dangerous or inappropriate activity, only if the conduct does not cease immediately after a mediation agreement has been reached.
4. All information required by court order will not be treated as confidential.
5. Any party may reveal the information necessary to defend against a formal complaint filed with the Mediation Oversight Committee or a judicial authority.

CR9. The mediator and all the parties must comply with the agreement to mediate. A noncompliance is subject to review by the Mediation Oversight Committee.

CR10. All parties must comply with the memorandum of agreement and the party confidentiality statement. If a problem arises with compliance, further mediation should be the first recourse. However, any noncompliance is subject to review by the Mediation Oversight Committee.

CR11. Any breach of the rules is subject to review by the Mediation Oversight Committee (MOC). The MOC has sole discretion to determine whether a breach occurred. All reprimands or other punitive action is the exclusive responsibility of the MOC within the confines of the Mediation Disciplinary Guidelines.

CR12. If a final judgment by the Mediation Oversight Committee concludes that a beach of the mediation rules did occur, a record of the incident will be included in the employee personnel file. If the MOC does not find that a breach occurred, no record will be placed in the employee personnel file. No action taken by the MOC is "public" information.

CR13. All actions by the MOC must be applied evenhandedly and objectively. No actual or apparent favoritism or discrimination may exist in decision making.

CR14. In the case that a breach of the mediation rules did occur, the MOC and the organization must attempt to repair any damage caused by the breach. The MOC may require the responsible party to make reasonable amends.

CR15. All complaints filed or information provided to the Mediation Oversight Committee are confidential. All members of the MOC will be held to the highest standard. A breach of any mediation rule by a member of the MOC will carry the strictest penalty.

Mediation Disciplinary Guidelines

The following Mediation Disciplinary Guidelines are to be used by the Mediation Oversight Committee (MOC). Disciplinary action will be taken when the MOC has determined if a breach of the mediation rules has occurred. Prior to any disciplinary action, the MOC must perform a comprehensive review and hold a private meeting to hear the complaint and response. The MOC will make a determination based on the information provided.

The MOC can and should offer creative and nonpunitive options for resolving the complaint. Alternative options must be less stringent than the measures set forth by the guidelines.

In the case that a breach of the mediation rules did occur, the MOC and the organization must attempt to repair any damage caused by the breach. The MOC may require the responsible party to make reasonable amends. Reparations for a breach can include any rational nonpunitive measure that effectively mends the damage.

The ultimate goal of discipline in the context of mediation is to repair injury and prevent a further breach—in essence, to rehabilitate. Punitive measures are appropriate and necessary, but only inasmuch as they affect rehabilitation. In certain extreme cases, the necessary course of action will be solely punitive. These disciplinary guidelines will help instruct the MOC in making just determinations. The MOC must also be committed to thoughtful and thorough evaluation of every situation; trust in the MOC is imperative for the success of the mediation process.

Punitive Measures

The matrix illustrated in Table 1 will help guide the MOC in making disciplinary determinations. A breach of the mediation rules will be punished according to the level of the offense, in conjunction with the number of similar offenses that have occurred. Each punitive action is combined with a probationary period. A repeat offense during a probationary period will result in a more severe punishment. After the requisite probationary period has expired, any new offense will be evaluated as if it were the first offense.

All reprimands will be recorded in the employee personnel file for the probationary period. When the probationary period has expired, the record will be removed from the file. In addition to the reprimands listed here, probationary periods will be subject to the policy requirements and restrictions of the organization.

The MOC can implement creative nonpunitive options or impose less stringent punishment for these offenses, only if there is no actual or apparent favoritism or discrimination. Alternative options must be less stringent than the measures set forth by the guidelines. All actions by the MOC must be applied evenhandedly and objectively.

The list on the following page represents some of the more common, yet serious, breaches of the mediation rules. Generally speaking, these are the appropriate punitive measure for each breach, according to level. This list is not all-inclusive, nor is it necessarily the only action that the MOC may take for a similar offense. The circumstances of each offense must be weighed by the MOC in order to ensure a just and evenhanded result.

Table 1
Disciplinary Chart

Action: Probation:	Verbal Reprimand 90 Days	Written Reprimand 1 Year	3 Day Suspension 3 Years	5 Day Suspension Permanent	Discharge
Level I	1st Offense	2nd Offense	3rd Offense	4th Offense	5th Offense
Level II		1st Offense	2nd Offense	3rd Offense	4th Offense
Level III			1st Offense	2nd Offense	3rd Offense
Level IV				1st Offense	2nd Offense
Level V					1st Offense

1. A breach of CR4, negotiating dishonestly or in bad faith, or taking unfair advantage of another person, is a Level II offense.

2. A breach of CR5, using the mediation process to intimidate, harass, threaten, manipulate, or harm the reputation of a person, is a Level II offense.

3. A breach of CR6, using the mediation process to reprimand or punish, is a Level II offense.

4. A breach of CR7, a breach of confidentiality by the mediator, is a Level III offense.

5. A breach of CR8, a breach of confidentiality by a party, is a Level II offense.

6. A breach of CR10, noncompliance with the mediation agreement, is a Level II offense.

7. A breach of CR13, favoritism or discrimination in decision making by a member of the Mediation Oversight Committee, is a Level III offense and requires immediate dismissal from the MOC.

8. A breach of CR 15, a breach of confidentiality by a member of the Mediation Oversight Committee, is a Level III offense and requires immediate dismissal from the MOC.

9. Any serious offense committed by a member of the Board of Mediators will result in dismissal from the BOM in addition to the appropriate punitive measures.

10. Any serious offense committed by a member of the Mediation Oversight Committee will result in dismissal from the MOC in addition to the appropriate punitive measures.

11. Any serious offense similar to the ones described above, committed by a Board of Directors member who is also serving on the Mediation Oversight Committee or the Board of Mediators, will result in dismissal from the Board of Directors.

12. Any breach not described above must be reviewed by the MOC. Prior to any disciplinary action, the MOC must perform a comprehensive review and hold a private meeting to hear the complaint and response. An appropriate punitive measure will then be determined by the MOC.

Appendix A

Agreement to Mediate

Agreement to Mediate

I understand that the purpose of mediation is to find a mutually acceptable solution. I intend to discuss the issues openly and honestly and negotiate in good faith. I understand that mediation must never be used to take unfair advantage of another person. Under no circumstances will I use what I learn in mediation in order to intimidate, harass, threaten, manipulate, or harm the reputation of a person.

I understand that a mediator facilitates communication between the parties and will remain impartial at all times. The mediator does not act in the capacity of a lawyer or a judge and does not offer legal advice or legal representation.

I agree that all written and verbal communication related to the mediation will remain confidential and will not be disclosed without the written permission of all the parties. I understand that no information obtained from mediation will be used by the employer or any employee to reprimand or punish. I acknowledge the exceptions as follows:

- According to organization policy, the mediator or any party may reveal information related to behavior prohibited by law, such as discriminatory or criminal activity.
- Any party may reveal to the Mediation Oversight Committee information related to behavior prohibited by formal organization policy, such as dangerous or inappropriate activity, only if the conduct does not cease immediately after a mediation agreement has been reached.
- All information required by court order will not be treated as confidential.
- The mediator or any party may reveal the information necessary to defend against a formal complaint filed with the Mediation Oversight Committee or a judicial authority.

I know that the mediator or any party has the right to terminate the mediation if further discussion will not be productive.

I understand that participating in mediation does not preclude any person from using an alternative grievance procedure or the legal system if the dispute is not mutually resolved.

Finally, I have read and agree to comply with all of the mediation rules, as well as, the spirit and intent of mediation.

Name:	Job Title:
Signature:	Date:
Name:	Job Title:
Signature:	Date:

Appendix B

Mediation Request Form

Mediation Request Form

- The purpose of mediation is to find a mutually acceptable solution.

- Issues will be discussed openly, honestly, and in good faith.

- Mediation must never be used to take unfair advantage of another person.

- Mediation will not be used to intimidate, harass, threaten, manipulate, or harm the reputation of a person.

- The mediator facilitates communication and will remain impartial at all times.

- All discussions will remain confidential.

Your contact information:

Name:	Job Title:
Work Phone Number:	Home Phone Number:
Work Address:	

Give a brief description of the conflict:

Name the people who you expect will participate in mediation:

Name:	Work Phone:
Work Address:	
Name:	Work Phone:
Work Address:	
Signature:	*Date:*

Appendix C

Memorandum of Agreement

Memorandum of Agreement

This Memorandum of Agreement explains in detail the settlement that we have reached. It includes all the pertinent information needed to understand and comply with our agreement. With this agreement, we make a promise in good faith to comply with all the requirements and restrictions of our compromise. If for any reason it becomes impossible to fulfil any aspect of this contract, we agree to discuss the obstacle immediately and make mutually acceptable modifications.

The final section of this Memorandum is a *Party Confidentiality Statement*. This statement outlines in detail any issues that we agree to make "public." All mediation discussions and resolutions will be kept completely confidential, with the exception of the items described in the Party Confidentiality Statement.

We understand that any breach of this Memorandum of Agreement and the Party Confidentiality Statement is strictly prohibited by the mediation rules.

Name:	Job Title:
Signature:	Date:
Name:	Job Title:
Signature:	Date:

References

American Bar Association. (1982). *Alternative Dispute Resolution: Who's in Charge of Mediation*. Washington, DC: Author.

———. (1984). *Divorce and Family Mediation*. Chicago, IL: ABA Press.

———. (1990). *Family Dispute Resolution: Options for All Ages*. Washington, DC: Author.

Baruch Bush, R. A., with Folger, J. P. (1994). *The Promise of Mediation: Responding to Conflict Through Empowerment and Recognition*. San Francisco, CA: Jossey-Bass.

Bastress, R., & Harbaugh, J. (1990). *Interviewing, Counseling, and Negotiating*. Boston, MA: Little, Brown and Company.

Becvar, D. S., & Becvar, R. J. (1996). *Family Therapy: A Systemic Integration* (3rd ed.). Needham Heights, MA: Allyn and Bacon.

Bucklew, N. (1997). *Faculty Mediation Program: West Virginia University*. Morgantown: West Virginia University.

Community Mediation Center. (1989). *Mediation and Conflict Resolution*. Harrisonburg, VA: Author.

Corey, G. (1996). *Theory and Practice of Counseling and Psychotherapy* (5th ed.). Pacific Grove, CA: Brooks/Cole Publishing Company.

Domenici, K. (1996). *Mediation: Empowerment in Conflict Management*. Prospect Heights, IL: Waveland Press.

Dunlop, J. T., with Zack, A. M. (1997). *Mediation and Arbitration of Employment Disputes*. San Francisco, CA: Jossey-Bass.

Fisher, R., & Ertel, D. (1995). *Ready to Negotiate: The Getting to Yes Workbook*. New York: Penguin.

Fisher, R., & Ury, W. (1991). *Getting to Yes*. New York: Penguin.

Folberg, J., with Taylor, A. (1984). *Mediation: A Comprehensive Guide to Resolving Conflicts Without Litigation*. San Francisco, CA: Jossey-Bass.

Ford Foundation. (1978). *Social Conflict*. New York: Author.

Goldberg, B., Sander, F., & Rogers, N. (1999). *Dispute Resolution: Negotiation, Mediation, and Other Processes*. New York: Aspen Publishers.

Goodman, A. (1994). *Basic Skills for the New Mediator.* Rockville, MD: Solomon Publications.

Haynes, J. (1994). *The Fundamentals of Family Mediation.* New York: SUNY Press.

Hodge, B. J., & Anthony, W. P. (1988). *Organization Theory.* Needham Heights, MA: Allyn and Bacon.

Irving, H., & Benjamin, M. (1995). *Family Mediation: Contemporary Issues.* Thousand Oaks, CA: Sage Publications

Kestner, P. (ed.). (1988). *Education and Mediation: Exploring the Alternatives.* Washington, DC: American Bar Association.

Kheel, T. (1999). *The Keys to Conflict Resolution: Proven Methods of Settling Disputes Voluntarily.* New York: Four Walls Eight Windows.

Kilpatrick, A. C., & Holland, T. P. (1995). *Working with Families: An Integrative Model by Level of Functioning.* Needham Heights, MA: Allyn and Bacon.

Kolb, D. K. (1997). *When Talk Works: Profiles of Mediators.* San Francisco, CA: Jossey-Bass.

Kovach, K. K. (1994). *Mediation: Principles and Practice.* St. Paul, MN: West.

Levine, S. (1989). *Getting to Resolution: Turning Conflict into Collaboration.* San Francisco, CA: Berrett-Koehler Publishers.

Lovenhein, P. (1996). *How to Mediate Your Dispute.* Berkeley, CA: Nolo.com.

McDermott, E. P., & Berkeley, A. E. (1996). *Alternative Dispute Resolution in the Workplace.* Westport, CT: Greenwood Publishing Group.

Moore, C. W. (1996). *The Mediation Process: Practical Strategies for Resolving Conflict.* San Francisco, CA: Jossey-Bass.

National Association of Social Workers. (1995). *Standards of Practice for Social Work Mediators.* [Brochure]. Washington, DC: Author.

Newfield, N. A. (personal communication, January 1998; February 2000).

Patrick, T. (1996). *State Bar Basic Mediation Training.* Morgantown, WV: Author.

Patrick, T. (personal communication, January 1998).

Patton, B. R., Giffin, K., & Nyquist Patton, E. (1989). *Decision-Making Group Interaction* (3rd ed.). New York: HarperCollins Publishers.

Potter, B. (1996). *From Conflict to Cooperation: How to Mediate a Dispute.* Berkeley, CA: Ronin Publishing.

Prather, V. (ed.). (1990). *Family Dispute Resolution.* Washington, DC: American Bar Association.

Rothman, J. (1995). *A Lawyer's Practical Guide to Mediation.* Kearney, NE: Morris.

Rules of Procedure for Court-Annexed Mediation in the Circuit Courts of West Virginia. (1993).

Schein, E. H. (1980). *Organizational Psychology* (3rd ed.). Englewood Cliffs, NJ: Prentice-Hall.

Schwerin, E. (1995). *Mediation, Citizen Empowerment, and Transformational Politics.* Westport, CT: Praeger.

Slaikeu, K. A. (1995). *When Push Comes to Shove: A Practical Guide to Mediating Disputes.* San Francisco, CA: Jossey-Bass.

Slaikeu, K. A., & Hasson, R. H. (1998). *Controlling the Costs of Conflict: How to Design a System for Your Organization.* San Francisco, CA: Jossey-Bass.

St. Antoine, T. J. (1998). *The Common Law of the Workplace: The Views of Arbitrators.* Washington, DC: BNA Books.

Stein, M., with Ernst, D. J. (1997). *Resolving Conflict Once and for All: A Practical How-To Guide to Mediating Disputes.* Louisville, KY: Mediation First.

U.S. Department of Justice. (1996). *Conflict Resolution Education.* Washington, DC: Author.

Walsh, F. (ed.). (1993). *Normal Family Processes.* New York: The Guilford Press.

Yarn, D. H. (ed). (1999). *Dictionary of Conflict Resolution.* San Francisco, CA: Jossey-Bass.

Index

About the Author

REBECCA JANE WEINSTEIN is an attorney and social worker. Her experience includes serving as executive director of the West Virginia Center for Dispute Resolution, a nonprofit organization dedicated to peaceful, nonviolent conflict resolution. She is also a former labor and employment lawyer, who represented members of the National Education Association in West Virginia. The owner of Mediation Alternatives, a mediation practice and training firm, she continues to pioneer alternative conflict resolution and mediation efforts.